The Pricing

Jan Y. Yang

The Pricing Puzzle

How to Understand and Create Impactful Pricing for Your Products

 Springer

Jan Y. Yang
Simon-Kucher & Partners
Cologne, Germany

ISBN 978-3-030-50776-3   ISBN 978-3-030-50777-0   (eBook)
https://doi.org/10.1007/978-3-030-50777-0

This Springer imprint is published by the registered company Springer Nature Switzerland AG.
The registered company address is: Gewerbestrasse 11, 6330 Cham, Switzerland

To my life companion and adoring wife Doreen for her unrelenting support and patience over all these years, to whom I am deeply indebted

Foreword

This book is a treasure trove of pricing tactics illustrated by real-life examples. And even more importantly, Jan Yang looks behind the scenes and offers his analysis on various pricing stories that he personally collected over the years. While observing the world through the lens of a pricing consultant, he puts himself in the shoes of business leaders and consumers in his pricing narratives.

Business leaders should take pricing seriously, because price is undisputedly the most important driver of profit and enterprise value. Price management goes far beyond setting prices. Instead, price management should be seen as active value management. Common practices like cost-plus pricing or following the competition are ill-fated. In doing so, one effectively no longer takes part in the quest for excellence. Failure to act on the heterogeneity of customers leads to mediocrity, the fate of a price taker. Even more importantly, business leaders should take pricing seriously because of the net present value of pricing. The fact is that no matter how great a product is, it has a finite shelf life. During this limited window of opportunity, the prime years will contribute the lion's share to revenue and profits, while residual value toward the end of this time period threatens to fall swiftly. Therefore, it is imperative for any business to get pricing right early on.

For their own benefit, consumers should not be beating themselves up with the price they pay. As Benjamin Franklin said, "*Bitterness of poor quality remains long after the sweetness of low price is forgotten*." Price serves as a yardstick of value, especially when consumers have little knowledge of the product or service in question. Life is short. Do not let the price get in your way. You have many more important things to regret than having paid a little too much. As a matter of fact, there is ample empirical evidence suggesting that people are willing to pay extra in exchange for "*peace of mind*".

At the end of the day, customers only make the purchase when the perceived value of the goods in question is equal to or greater than the sacrifice, which is the price they have to pay. It is a kind of equivalence that businesses can search for through repeated trial and error, or by means of a more structured price finding method. The value added by pricing consultants lies in helping one to find the sweet spot of the price-value equilibrium more reliably and quickly. A pricing consultant can also help unravel hidden gems that customers value greatly and have a high willingness to pay for.

The trio of business leaders, consumers, and pricing consultants provides answers to the pricing puzzle that entangles our life. Enjoy the pricing stories which chronicle Jan's observations and reflections along his pricing journey of more than a decade. You will encounter your own eureka moments in reading this book and hopefully find solutions to your own pricing puzzle.

Simon-Kucher & Partners   Prof. Dr. Dr. h.c. mult. Hermann Simon
Bonn, Germany
Summer of 2020

Acknowledgments

I am grateful to colleagues at Simon-Kucher & Partners, in particular Xiao-Min Tung, Florence Wang, and Haotian Zhang for their contribution to the write-up of several pricing stories with their research, creativity, and suggestions.

I thank my editors Dr. Prashanth Mahagaonkar and Ruth Milewski for their genuine interest in my book from the very beginning and their helpful suggestions along the way.

Last but not least, I am indebted to Prof. Dr. Dr. h.c. mult. Hermann Simon, Honorary Chairman at Simon-Kucher & Partners, who inspired me from day one to go on my own "pricing journey," and who reviewed the manuscript of this book.

Contents

Oh Price: Prelude

When I embarked on the flight for my first-ever pricing project in Toronto in the summer of 2008, I did not see that it was the first step in a long pricing journey still ahead. My job as a pricing consultant took me to many different places. Following my first assignments in Canada, I have been to almost all major European countries, a couple in the Middle East, to then go all the way to East and Southeast Asia. I am under the impression that I have spent more time up in the air than on the ground. Along the way, in both time and space, I have learned to observe and interpret the world through the lenses of a pricing consultant.

Price has been an indispensable instrument for human society since the introduction of division of labor and the exchange of products and services. In an ideal world, the value (the utility) must equate or exceed the price (the sacrifice) in order for a transaction to take place. It is most evident when it comes to a product, about which one has little knowledge, where price serves as a yardstick of value. Benjamin Franklin, one of the Founding Fathers of the United States and a polymath, once said: "*Bitterness of poor quality remains long after the sweetness of low price is forgotten.*" The older I become, the more inclined I am to buy more expensive or higher-value products, whenever I have the choice.

Price plays a role in every decision in modern times. No matter whether you want it or not, price is there, everywhere. The only thing that one cannot put a price tag on is probably time. Everything else has a price. Imagine you go on a trip. Starting from booking air or train tickets, you encounter all kinds of price tags along the way, be it those for hotel rooms, the airport shuttle, meals in restaurants, and refreshments in kiosks or automatic vending

© Springer Nature Switzerland AG 2020

J. Y. Yang, *The Pricing Puzzle*, https://doi.org/10.1007/978-3-030-50777-0_1

machines, just to name a few. What I find fascinating are the minibar menus in five-star hotels in China. The price for a bag of nuts or a beer can vary so wildly even within the same city that the price setting process because of this appears to be completely arbitrary. Among others, older high-class hotels tend to have higher price tags on the minibar items. I would guess that what I see is reflective of a price legacy. Back in the old days, the majority of hotel guests were foreigners who had much deeper pockets than the average Chinese guest. The high-class hotels logically stocked imported snacks and drinks in the minibars to capture foreign guests' higher willingness to pay. While the outside world moves on with the prices of imported foods dropping significantly, the menus of hotel minibars were forgotten in the tailwind of history.

Prices tell stories, intriguing stories. I take notes or pictures whenever I spot an interesting pricing practice. In this book, you will find 24 pricing stories which document my observations and reflections along my pricing journey of the last decade. A decent number of the stories happened in China, a price wonderland in which I, as both consumer and pricing consultant, have observed unconventional pricing practices which were a rarity elsewhere, such as the frequent asking of insanely low prices among tech unicorns. It is not uncommon for ambitious startups to pay consumers to use their products. Wonder why? You will find some clues in this book.

Deep down, I want this book to be a fun, light read for just everybody so that I shall start with relatively easy-to-digest stories that consumers can readily relate to as connected to their own daily life. As the book progresses, I touch on more advanced topics that are probably more relevant for business owners and marketers. I conclude the book with some thoughts on the philosophical aspect of pricing to reconcile my conflicting roles as a consumer and a pricing consultant.

When discussing the nature of management,[1] Peter F. Drucker concluded that the single most important thing to remember about any enterprise is that there are no results inside of its walls. The aim of a business is to have satisfied customers. The aim of a hospital is a healed patient, that of a school is a student who has learned something and puts it to work ten years later. Inside an enterprise, there are only cost centers. Results exist only on the outside.

To that end, pricing should be taken seriously, because price is undisputedly the most important lever to drive the results on the outside. Numbers don't lie. Once a coffee shop franchise owner shared with me his moment of pricing enlightenment. When he was running business cases for the franchise, he happened to realize that an increase of one Chinese Yuan on the signature

---

[1] https://hbr.org/1988/09/management-and-the-worlds-work.

drink in the menu would shorten the break-even period for the franchisees by a whole month. No other levers have such a magnitude of impact on return on investment. It pays off to manage price actively. There are companies out there doing that every day, applying a variety of pricing strategies and tools.

In this book, I offer you an opportunity to look behind the scenes of curious pricing stories. I do not pretend to be able to explain everything. As the German philosopher Hegel once said: what is rational is real; and what is real is rational. There is always a valid reason why a certain pricing practice exists. Based on my observations and reflections, you, dear readers, have all the freedom to decide how to interpret it for yourself. Although I often refer to consumers when discussing pricing phenomena, the principles apply to B2B business too.

Let's put on these pricing glasses and get started. I hope that you will find joy and enlightenment in my pricing narratives.

Dr. Jan Y. Yang

Pricing enthusiast and evangelist

Summer 2019, Shanghai/Spring 2020, Ingelheim am Rhein

The Power of Choice

What You Will Discover?

Almost in every city in the world, there is a bar street, where you will find all kinds of bars to choose from in a concentrated area. Don't the owners know that there will be more competition if they are so close to each other? Now take a moment and reflect on your own shopping preference. Would you prefer a store with a big assortment or a small one? People like to have choices. What does it mean for business? Does it mean the more the merrier?

In 2000, psychologists Sheena Iyengar and Mark Lepper from Columbia and Stanford University conducted a study about how people shop jams. The researchers set up a jam table in an upscale food market. On one day, there were 24 different jams on display. One another day, there were only six jams. What is the impact on the purchase decision of customers by varying the number of choices? Three key findings are illustrated below in Fig. 1.

Finding 1 A larger variety is conducive to soliciting more attraction. 60% of the customers stopped by the jam table when there were 24 jams on display, whereas the stop-by ratio dropped to 40% when there were only six jams. The result is intuitive, as retailers always try to have their shelves fully stocked with a variety of products.

Finding 2 The number of choices has little bearing on the propensity for try-outs. The average number of jams tasted was on about the same level for both groups, with Group B having a slightly better result.

© Springer Nature Switzerland AG 2020

J. Y. Yang, *The Pricing Puzzle*, https://doi.org/10.1007/978-3-030-50777-0_2

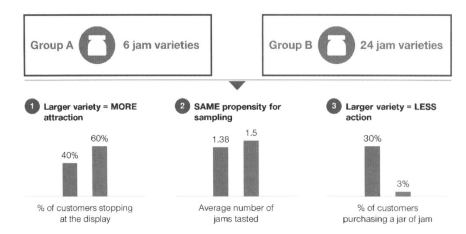

Fig. 1 Key findings of the jams study by Iyengar and Lepper, 2000. (Source: Iyengar, Lepper, 2000; Group A: $n = 260$, Group B: $n = 242$; Compiled by the author)

Finding 3 This is THE moment of truth. Although the large variety of 24 jams does perform better in attracting the potential buyer's attention (stopby) and stimulating interest (try-out), it does not translate into a higher sales conversion rate. In the case of six jam variety, 30% customers bought a jam. However, in the case of 24 jam variety, only 10% customers picked a jam. What counts in the end are realized sales. The limited number of choices achieved superior results, by far.

To sum it up: the study above unraveled a so-called "*more is less*" phenomenon in customers' shopping behavior, also known as the "*paradox of choice*." When confronted with too many choices, consumers tend to be paralyzed by these and shy away from purchase decisions, to the detriment of the retailers.

Compared to material goods such as jams, the "*paradox of choice*" phenomenon is of even greater relevance in the service sector. While the service providers enjoy a greater degree of liberty and latitude in creating new offers, they are also burdened with finding the right product at the right price for their customers. And unavoidably, pricing then gets more entangled with product design in the service sector. A solid understanding of customer needs and their willingness to pay for having these needs fulfilled underscores the necessity of a successful monetization of the offers. In this light, service companies should productize a price instead of pricing a product.

In particular, the verticals with heavy upfront investment and little marginal cost are genuinely more concerned with pricing, as there is little room for cost optimization for them. The telecommunication industry is a case in point. Telecom companies all over the world face a twofold challenge. On the one hand, they have to continuously make investment into technologies which are set to be superseded by newer generations of technologies in a few years. On the other hand, to differentiate oneself from competitors is somewhat difficult, as the customers are inclined to see all telecom products as me-too products.

During the pricing project for a leading telecommunications company, we were analyzing the historical tariffs, which typically consisted of different levels of allowances for call minutes, mobile data volume/speed, a set of Internet bandwidth, and value-adding services. We found many legacy tariffs that the client had created in promotion campaigns over the years without there being meaningful variance in specifications. In fact, in the course of technological upgrades at telecom companies, it is not uncommon that some old tariffs are automatically paired with better specifications than contractually agreed upon.

I also benefited from a windfall once. Years ago, I signed a contract for a landline and an Internet connection with a telecom company. The Internet connection had a download speed of 20 MB/second, specified in the contract, which was not bad at that time. The provider some time later stopped providing the 20 MB/second speed option, as 100 MB/second had become the standard in the market, while 50 MB/second became the lowest speed option. As an incumbent customer, I received a free upgrade to 50B/second without additional cost. I don't know whether the service provider had done the math. My guess is that the provider could have charged a few more euros for the unsolicited upgrade, without any churns. It is unlikely that the legacy customers would have gotten cheaper deals somewhere else. However, I don't know of a single case where telecom companies have charged legacy customers for such upgrades. On a separate note, even if the telecom companies do not raise the prices for a forced upgrade, they could profit from communicating the good news to their customers. Retention efforts often fail, because they are passive instead of active. Companies fail to seize the right moment for communicating something great for customers like this.

When digging into the past promotion campaigns, we found an interesting cohort of so-called build-your-own (BYO) tariffs. In these tariffs, the customers could freely specify the exact level of call minutes, data allowance, value-added services, etc. The product management thought BYO was a brilliant idea to quell the customers' desire to have their individual needs fulfilled; therefore they ran several BYO campaigns in the past years. Analysis showed that the take rate was mediocre, as the share of BYO contracts remained negligible. It was more revealing to find out that more than 60% of the tariffs that the customers had created were already available in existing product portfolios, while another 20% BYO tariffs were not significantly different from pre-defined tariffs. These BYO customers made the superfluous effort of designing their tariffs thereby, in a sense, reinventing the wheel for nothing. The market research we conducted later on during the project also proved the lack of creativity of customers when it came to the customization of the tariffs.

Not limited to telecommunications industry, I have seen similar patterns in many other service verticals. The truth is: no matter how badly customers want to have choices, they agonize over decisions. It is generally not a good idea to give the customers the full liberty of configuring their own offers. When it comes to BYO tariffs, empirical evidence suggests that the majority of the customers actually have no clue about how to build a tariff. The few who do know how to do this constitute a profit leakage for the service provider, as they optimize their tariffs according to their needs and avoid paying extra money. There is another severe caveat for the service providers. By offering BYO, they thus reveal the unit price of a stand-alone service, which could raise unpleasant questions about the price integrity of existing tariffs, by no means a desirable side effect. But as we have learned from the jam study, it is still wise to give the customers the impression that they are well-informed about purchase decisions. What might be a better alternative? When browsing for a new internet service provider for our new home earlier this year, I bumped into a service provider which provides an interactive session on its product website (See Fig. 2). It asked the question:

"How many devices from the following list do you have at home?"

After specifying the connected devices by category, I was shown, in real time, the minimum required bandwidth and recommended bandwidth, which in my personal constellation above, was 100 MB/second and 200 MB/second, respectively. In this kind of setup, the customer reveals information important to making the right decision. In return, she/he is rewarded by being given an individualized product recommendation. It is a win-win situation powered by choice. Leading companies around the world use similar

Fig. 2 Interactive guide to product selection on the website of a telecommunications company. (Source: Author's own figure)

techniques to entice customers to reveal their preferences. You may not recognize these at once, since they are hiding in plain sight.

Let's take a look at another example. In most videos you watch on YouTube, there is this little "skip" button appearing at the right-bottom corner of the video which allows the viewer to reject the advertisement. Why would YouTube do such a thing? Would it not be better to force the viewers to watch the ads to the end? Maybe, but it opens new doors of possibilities in giving the viewers the choice to skip an ad that they do not like. The time after which the viewer hits the skip button also provides valuable insights for the advertiser. If the skip happens at 5 seconds sharp, you know that the viewer was merely counting the seconds and not really paying attention to the content, or the content was not appealing to her/him. If the skip button is pressed later, the odds are that the video has aroused interest in the viewer to a certain extent. In effect, the elapse of time till the skip button is hit is indicative of the quality of the ad. We are now used to the skip button. But until recently, it was a black box to the advertisers regarding how the ads were perceived by the viewers, as the ads used to be charged mainly on depending on the number of clicks.

Marketers used to believe that all viewers on a platform tend to be homogeneous. That may not be a safe assumption any longer. In light of the behavioral dynamics of the younger generations, I would argue that even though the users of a certain media platform tend to show a certain level of converging interests, there is no guarantee that this should reflect on their shopping behavior in any uniform way. Instead, it is becoming increasingly important for brands to have a more in-depth grasp of consumer characteristics. Instead of guessing what consumers want, the skip button allows and encourages them to reveal their true opinions.

The very existence of skip button also incentivizes the advertisers to improve the quality of their ads. YouTube's video recommendation mechanism used to give more weight to the click-through rate, which led to an exaggerated covering of videos. Over time, the recommendation mechanism has undergone changes in the composition of the criteria, such as assigning greater importance to playback completion, playback duration, attention, and the number of views. Advertisers producing good content are prioritized in the recommendations made by YouTube. So it can be a win-win-win situation for advertisers, viewers, as well as YouTube.

Individualism is the epitome of today's consumerism. Customization on an individual level or a differentiation among customer segments is of growing importance for companies in order to retain customers and extract deserved value. However, companies often fail in creating customized offers. There are no universal truths as regards the granularity and degree of customization. It appears to be an attractive idea to let customer create the offers. In reality, as we can see from the BYO case of the telecom company, it does not work like that. Customers will be at sea when given too many choices, although we all claim that we like to have choices. It is the paradox of choice.

The good news is that this is a paradox that we can resolve. There are two givens in the equation: (A) customers like choices and (B) customers do not know how to make choices. The gap between the two is the lack of knowledge of the product or service in question; hence a lack of knowledge about how a customer's needs can be better fulfilled. A sound understanding of the use cases can effectively bridge the gap. The Internet service provider in the example abovementioned did not ask how big a bandwidth I needed (I truly had no clue). Instead, it asked how many connected devices there were in my household, which was the decisive question for then making the right choice. It is a smart tactic, considering that the majority of the competitors merely highlighted the recommended tariff in the product lineup without any further explanation. It was especially meaningless to have the middle option tagged as being the "*recommended tariff.*" When a customer feels unsure, she or he would settle for the middle option anyways. The less prior knowledge the customers have about the product or service in question, the more critical it becomes that the service provider knows what questions to ask to gauge customers' needs.

Remember This!

- Customers like choices, but they do not know how to make choices.
- The cognitive conundrum can be resolved by asking customers the right questions in a smart way.
- The more you know about a customer's use case, the greater the odds that you will be able to come up with a product that makes the customer happy.

The Color of Pricing

What You Will Discover?

It goes without saying that price discrimination is undesired as well as illegal in most countries. That being said, consumers may embrace price differentiation, provided that it comes with a legit rationale. Smart manufacturers create and price their products differently to cater to the needs of different customer segments. One possible dimension of price differentiation is based on gender. For similar products, should manufacturers charge higher prices for male or female customers? Will the answer differ by geography?

Pink for her, blue for him, as the cliché goes. Especially when it comes to infants, the color dominance is prevalent in all cultures which I am familiar with. I abhor clichés, so does my wife. On purpose, we dress our little boys in pink or other warm colors from time to time. And we do get questions from passersby in the public like: "*Cute kiddo. A girl, no?*"

"*Hm, nope.*" Usually this ends the awkward conversation and we move on.

Social norms permeate our lives. Not only do they dictate what colors are representative of which gender, but they also insinuate how the prices of the same or similar products should differ by gender, provided that underlying products are meant primarily either for her or for him. So women or men come to pay different prices for beauty and personal care products. While price discrimination is illegal in almost all jurisdictions, price differentiation is legit and broadly used by smart sellers to take advantage of the varying degrees of willingness to pay inherent in different customer groups.

The Chinese market for beauty and personal care products has been growing fast. Currently the second biggest in the world, it is likely to overtake the United States soon in terms of overall spending on beauty products, thanks to

© Springer Nature Switzerland AG 2020

J. Y. Yang, *The Pricing Puzzle*, https://doi.org/10.1007/978-3-030-50777-0_3

its rising younger, more affluent middle class with an increased appetite for luxury beauty and care products.[1] Especially women from tier 3–4 cities are seen as the driving force behind this increase in spending.[2] However, if women are willing to spend more on beauty and personal care, how does this manifest itself in the prices for products within this particular market?

Revelations in Germany

Triggered by the same question, an earlier price comparison study conducted by my colleagues in Germany showed that women paid on average 25% more in comparison to men for quasi-similar beauty products. In particular, the price difference between the female and male version of a perfume could amount to as much as an 80% premium for women. Consequently, also known as gender pricing, the topic of price differentiation based on gender has caught the attention of general media and is met with rage and claims of unfairness from consumers. However, the concept of price differentiation in and of itself is nothing new, considering its wide application in industries such as aviation, where it is widely accepted that one's flight ticket might have been more expensive than your neighbor's on the same flight.

Reality Check in China

To see whether and how gender pricing prevails in China, we conducted a replica of the original study and researched various beauty product types across different brands. See Fig. 1.

Similar to what was seen in Germany, we found an average price premium of 21% for women across several product types, including perfume, skincare, and haircare. In the meantime, we also discovered that it is not only women who pay a premium on beauty products in China. In fact, our study found that Chinese men also pay equal or even higher price premium for a male product variant that is seemingly similar to the corresponding female version in terms of functionality. Prices are on average 35% higher for men across certain distinct product types, such as deodorants and razors, as well as over-lapping product types, such as skincare and haircare. See Fig. 2.

---

[1] https://www.statista.com/topics/1897/cosmetics-in-china/.
[2] https://jingdaily.com/china-girl-power/.

Product type	Brand	Product name	Price for him	Price for her	Price difference
Perfume	Gucci	Gucci Guilty EdT 50ml	¥720	¥850	15%
	Gucci	Gucci Guilty Absolute EdP 50ml	¥720	¥850	15%
	Armani	Armani Code EdP 50ml	¥600	¥820	27%
	Prada	Prada L'Eau EdP 100ml	¥940	¥1,400	33%
Skincare	Shiseido	Shiseido Cleansing Foam 125ml	¥180	¥350	49%
	SK-II	SK-II Facial Cream Cleanser 120g	¥440	¥460	4%
	L'Oreal	L'Oreal Hydrating Serum	¥110	¥190	42%
	Nivea	Nivea Lipbalm 4.8g	¥29	¥35	17%
Haircare	L'Oreal	L'Oreal Anti-Dandruff Shampoo 400ml	¥45	¥46	2%
Make up	Sephora	Sephora Cushion	¥219	¥222	1%
					∅ = 21%

Fig. 1   Price comparison beauty and personal care products – female premium. (Source: Desk research, October 2019)

Product type	Brand	Product name	Price for him	Price for her	Price difference
Skincare	Shiseido	Shiseido Eye Cream 15ml	¥410	¥360	14%
	Unitouch	Unitouch Hydrating Facemasks 3pc	¥155	¥135	15%
	Nivea	Nivea Whitening Facial Cleanser 150ml	¥59	¥25	134%
	Biotherm	Biotherm Hydrating Toner 200ml	¥206	¥195	6%
	Sephora	Sephora Tone Up Cream 50ml	¥209	¥180	16%
	Doctor Li	Oil Control and Hydrating Mask 6pc	¥49	¥25	96%
Haircare	Syoss	Syoss Silicone Free Anti-Dandruff Shampoo 750ml	¥70	¥60	17%
Deodorant	Nivea	Nivea Invisible for Black & White Deodorant 50ml	¥39	¥35	11%
	Rexona	Rexona Antiperspirant Aerosol 150ml	¥32	¥27	18%
Razors	Gilette	Gillette Razor 3 Blades	¥32	¥26	24%
					∅ = 35%

Fig. 2   Price comparison beauty and personal care products – male premium. (Source: Desk research, October 2019)

So, Who Spends More? Men or Women?

It seems that the Chinese market for beauty and personal care exhibits some unique dynamics when it comes to gender pricing. What drives companies to make such price distinctions, and more specifically, which gender ends up paying more? There are several possible reasons for the opposing price differentiation findings in China.

On the one hand, when looking at the price premium on female beauty products, we can draw on the conventional knowledge that women have a higher willingness to pay for such products, which companies rightfully tap into when it comes to their pricing strategy. Nevertheless, as competition in the Chinese beauty and personal care market is intensifying due to a growing number of both domestic and international market players, women are becoming more well-informed, picky, and price-sensitive, which ultimately brings down prices and narrows the gender price gap. On the other hand, finding potential explanations for higher prices charged on men's products would be slightly more complicated.

First of all, price premium charged on men could be a reflection of particular characteristics of the Chinese male consumer base. Men who care more about their appearance are likely to be willing to spend more on beauty products than the average man. As such, their willingness to pay can be equal to or even higher than in women, especially when considering rather high-end, advanced beauty products that are not even found in the average women's beauty bag, such as a Shiseido eye cream (see Fig. 2). In fact, Chinese men's spending on facial products has grown 40% in 2018 compared to previous year.[3]

Secondly, willingness to pay for some beauty product types could be higher for men out of mere functionality or for reasons of necessity. This could explain the higher price on male versions of razors and deodorants. While the demand for these two product categories is generally lower in China, it is even lower among Chinese women than men.

Thirdly, companies could be positioning their product lines at different premium perceptions for men and women for competitive reasons. While the price level of a women's product line is under greater pressure from vying brands, the men's line can be positioned at a more premium level, where the competition is still less fierce.

Last but not least, women's usage of beauty products tends to outweigh that of their male counterparts, as a woman's beauty routine is usually more comprehensive and regular. This can be seen in the product configuration. For instance, Nivea's hydrating line for men consists of three simple steps,[4] whereas women are to purchase five products for the complete procedure.[5] Hence, the

---

[3] http://www.cbndata.com/report/1610/detail?isReading=report&page=5.
[4] https://item.jd.com/100001886799.html#crumb-wrap.
[5] https://item.jd.com/100000212589.html#crumb-wrap.

average total spending per person in a year, regardless of initial price differences, may fall within a small range in the end across genders.

Although beauty and personal care is an area that is conventionally female dominated, it seems that times are changing. Defying the cliché of masculinity, Chinese men are becoming more self-conscious and are starting to feel good about keeping their skin just as well cared for as their female counterparts. In recent years, we have been seeing an increasing number of beauty brands; international as well as local brands use male celebrities or key opinion leaders as brand ambassadors for their female product lines in China. In 2019 there were 24 such cases, up from 18 in 2018.[6] The shifting perception of men and beauty in China is set to provide beauty brands with more exciting opportunities for both product innovation and monetization.

Remember This!

- Clichés such as pink for her and blue for him do not have to remain static; and with these, price differentiation by gender may follow different rules in different parts of the world.
- Despite the conventional wisdom that females tend to have a higher willingness to pay for beauty products, there are exceptions where male consumers surpass the opposite gender in their quest for beauty.
- While it is easy to follow conventions, it is also worthwhile to look for exceptions that will translate into a higher willingness to pay and thereby profit!

---

[6] https://mp.weixin.qq.com/s/1Ocl1XVLdvdOpdK1V_Dm1w.

Good Morning Coffee

What You Will Discover?

We make decisions all the time. Our lives are shaped by the decisions we make. Price decisions have different dimensions for companies and consumers. For companies, price is the moment of truth in that price decisions ultimately drive results. For consumers, prices are paid reflective of solving a problem. One would genuinely believe that the lower the price, the better off the consumer, all else being equal. But is it really the case?

I am a heavy coffee drinker. I cannot start a day properly without a cup of coffee, no matter whether on work days or during leisure time. When I do not travel, the first thing I do when I get to the office is to go straight to the office kitchen to switch on the coffee machine. While it heats up, I go to my office, put away my stuff, and turn on the laptop. The moment I return to the kitchen, the coffee machine is ready for me to pour myself a double espresso. When I am out and about, I usually grab a coffee at a McDonald's restaurant or a convenience store in the morning.

However, such simple routines can sometimes become troublesome. A few years ago, I walked into a McDonald's restaurant in Suzhou for my wake-up coffee in the morning. I had had breakfast before I entered the restaurant. The motivation for entering that restaurant was as straightforward as a cup of black coffee, I swear. The coffee shopping turned out to be a bit trickier than I had thought.

The menu offered the following options:

- *McMuffin*: 6 RMB
- *Coffee*: 10 RMB
- *Breakfast combo* (which includes a McMuffin and a coffee): 6 RMB

© Springer Nature Switzerland AG 2020
J. Y. Yang, *The Pricing Puzzle*, https://doi.org/10.1007/978-3-030-50777-0_4

I rubbed my eye in disbelief and thought that I was probably daydreaming considering the 62.5% discount of the third option. The staff at the counter reaffirmed what I saw and recommended the breakfast combo for 6 RMB. I was conflicted over this. I would be punishing myself by choosing coffee over the breakfast combo. Who would pay more only to get less?

Two minutes later, the rational, or maybe not so rational, side of me got the upper hand. When I left the McDonald's restaurant, I was holding a cup of coffee on one hand and a McMuffin on the other. I gave myself a treat I did not deserve. As the McMuffin landed in my stomach, a feeling of regret arose. I should have known better.

It was rational of me to go for the combo for 6 RMB. Otherwise I would have paid 10 RMB for my coffee. Nevertheless, it was irrational of me to eat the McMuffin, from which my satisfaction rather decreased. The marginal gain from eating or drinking usually diminishes with amount. Just imagine you are stranded in a desert, running out of all supplies. If someone now brought you a glass of water, the amount of satisfaction would be immense. You would probably also appreciate the next two or three glasses as well, which would eventually quell your thirst. As you drink more, the amount of satisfaction would rise at a lesser rate. And, past a certain tipping point, satisfaction would turn into dissatisfaction. This is known as the law of diminishing returns. In that sense, the second bite of that other delicious McMuffin on that morning in Suzhou was my tipping point, unfortunately.

The breakfast combo is a price bundle. Bundling is a popular marketing tool that penetrates our daily lives, from restaurants, telecommunication plans, travel products, office software, cars to football matches, etc. Designing a good bundle is no easy task. On the one hand, one needs to identify the right ingredients to be bundled, which requires thorough analysis of consumer insights; on the other hand, one needs to find the right discount level to get to the best overall financial result. There is no panacea; every case merits its own solution. There are also occasions on which bundles are sold at premium in lieu of a discount, when the main product is so attractive that sellers can bundle-sell them with generally less popular products. The high willingness to pay for the sought-after product will spill over to other products.

If it were not for the fact that I had had breakfast earlier, I would have loved the McDonald's breakfast combo. It offers great value for consumers who are seeking easy and all-inclusive breakfast options. But my first instinct told me that the breakfast combo, which offered a whopping 63% discount, was priced wrong. By setting the bundle price to be that that of just the McMuffin, McDonald's practically gives away coffee for free and likely makes a loss on a stand-alone basis.

That said, I was able to make sense of such aggressive pricing behavior. The motivation may be twofold. Firstly, the breakfast combo may have been used to lure price-sensitive customers into the restaurant with a very low price and then earn money on other items. Secondly, it may serve a penetration strategy in the hope that the Chinese consumers will get used to Western-style breakfasts and cultivate customer loyalty and higher willingness to pay over time. To put things in perspective, McDonald's Germany also offers breakfast combos with discounts, which usually range between 20% and 30%.

Frankly speaking, I have little faith in both hypotheses. To begin with, there are not many items that McDonald's can cross-sell or up-sell in the morning. There are mainly muffins and hot drinks in the breakfast menu and a limited amount of side dishes that can be bundled. Even if the purpose is to foster a customer base leaning toward having a Western-style breakfast, the aggressive pricing strategy would not have been necessary. Until today, 2020, the breakfast combo still sells for 6 RMB, while almost all budget Chinese restaurants have increased the prices for breakfasts significantly in recent years, reaching up to more than 10 RMB for an average breakfast. The significant discount that comes with the McDonald's breakfast combo that used to signal a deal effect now turned into doubts over the food quality, which threatens to distance loyal customers over time. A discount available for long periods of time will shift the price anchor in consumers' minds. There is no easy going back once this has happened.

It is debatable whether all the price decisions, promotions, and campaigns at McDonald's are effective. Among the ill-designed ones, the persisting breakfast combo will definitely top my list.

Remember This!

- A good price decision (buying the breakfast combo instead of the coffee) can be detrimental to customer experience (eating the McMuffin while not hungry).
- Companies' price decisions need to evolve over time to keep abreast of market reality.
- A long-lasting discount is doomed to have a detrimental effect.

(In)dispensable Spicy Chicken Wings

What You Will Discover?

I touched upon the concept of bundling in the last story. In this story, I am going to go one step further and discuss how bundling works. *Spoiler alert*: you will encounter yet another McDonald's example, as it is a great platform to illustrate bundling-related topics. Bundling does not mean that you can just put any products together and then offer a feel-good discount. There is more to it. How does one design a meaningful product bundle? What are the guiding principles?

Well, I do not go to McDonald's only for coffee.

Notwithstanding all my dietary disciplines, I confess that I am big on fried chicken wings, especially those hot chicken wings at McDonald's. If I am correctly informed, McDonald's hot chicken wings are specifically made in, by, and for China.

To keep daily hassles at a minimum, I have trained myself to simplify routine decisions such as what to wear, where to eat, and what to eat to the largest extent possible. McDonald's is a preferred dining choice when I am on the road by my own. I know what I can expect at McDonald's, no matter where I am. And when it comes to McDonald's, in 90% of the cases, I will choose a Big Mac value menu, which consists of a Big Mac hamburger, a coke, and French fries. The Big Mac may sound boring, but it is a safe choice, and it is available everywhere. To see why that is the case, *The Economist* publishers use the Big Mac Index as an informal way of measuring the purchasing power parity (PPP) across countries. More often than not, I would swap fries for hot chicken wings by paying a bit of extra money. It is totally worth it.

In July 2019, I was on a business trip to Nanjing. After the job was done in the late morning, I cut myself some slack and took a walk around the scenic Xuanwu Lake in the city center. After half an hour or so, I started searching for lunch options and soon caught sight of a huge golden arch in front of me. It seemed to be my lucky day. Like I always did, I ordered my standard choice, i.e., the Big Mac value menu, at the counter and asked them to upgrade the fried chips to hot spicy chicken wings. The answer from the other side of the counter was a downright "no." Not seeing this coming, I was a bit irritated and countered: "What do you mean by, 'no'?"

It turned out that McDonald's no longer offered the option to trade up from fries to have chicken wings instead. I was astonished. Since I had set my mind on eating those delicious chicken wings, it would have been very disappointing for me, if not devastating, to leave without them.

Guess what? I sighed and in the end bought the value menu and the spicy chicken wings on top. I did not like the fries as much as I had expected and had to throw at least half of them away. Although I deliberately made the decision, I still felt ripped off. But at least the spicy chicken wings lived up to the expectation.

The next day, I headed back to the office in Shanghai and joked about my choosing the spicy chicken wings with my co-workers while standing by the water dispenser in the office kitchen. One colleague looked up at me and could not help revealing agitation. Then she told me that she happened to have been to a KFC (*Kentucky Fried Chicken*) restaurant near the office just yesterday and had also tried to get an upgrade to have chicken wings. Coincidentally, she had failed in this, too. KFC rejected her request to swap fries for chicken wings as well. She was also desperate to get the chicken wings so that she did the same thing as I had done – which was to buy a menu as well as the chicken wings. Well, she also threw away all the fries. Then I thought to myself, wow, kowtow to these masters of bundling, you played it well.

Bundling is a common practice in the fast-food industry, everywhere in the world. Last time you visited a McDonald's or KFC restaurant, you probably bought a value menu which was a bundle. To see why bundles are widely used in the fast food industry, let's take a closer look at McDonald's as an example: the Big Mac burger is the go-to product in McDonald's restaurants in almost all countries around the world, which the majority of consumers would consider buying. Their desire as well as willingness to pay for additional other products such as fries or soft drinks tends to be more diverse and generally lower.

McDonald's prices differ across countries (which explains why there is a Big Mac Index). The following analysis uses the prices in the United States for illustrative purpose. A Big Mac costs $3.99, a medium-sized serving of French fries $1.79, and a medium-sized soft drink $1.29. A consumer with a limited budget or one without a strong preference for side dish products would probably go for a single Big Mac, the *hero product* in pricing jargon, paying $3.99. However, there is a $5.99 Big Mac Meal which costs only $2 more than a stand-alone Big Mac, and it includes medium French fries and a soft drink which pricing consultants refer to as fillers. In principle, a bundle should be built around a hero product (it usually only makes sense to have more than one hero product in scenarios, where consumers are faced with a large variety of options, e.g., car equipment configuration) and complemented with fillers. Hero products are signature products that the majority of customers like to buy and are willing to pay for. Filler products are those that some customers, but not all, like to have, and the willingness to pay for these differs to a considerable extent. As a rule of thumb, you need one hero and a few fillers to make a good bundle. By offering a moderate discount, the merchant entices a customer to purchase a bundle which contains some filler products that she or he otherwise would not buy on a stand-alone basis.

The Big Mac value menu looks like a good deal for the consumer. Among others, the engineered menu price of $5.99 appears visually less pricey thanks to the 0.99 price ending, which is a proven trick that finds broad application in fast-moving consumer goods. Yet, the decisive question for McDonald's is whether the gain from cross-selling additional products outweighs the sacrifice of giving discounts on the bundle. If you do the math, you will notice that the discount is moderate, just 15%. In the last story, I talked about the impaired efficacy of McDonald's China's long-lasting discount on the breakfast combo. It is too obvious that there is something off with the combo price, as it is easy for any living being to calculate. In contrast, the discounts of the other McDonald's value menus are not easy to work out. Consumers just assume that these are good deals for them in general. In other words, McDonald's has framed consumers in its favor by means of making consistent offers of value menus and communicating these.

Yet, the ultimate question remains: What does it mean for McDonald's if a customer trades up from purchasing just a single Big Mac to having the value menu? It depends on the profit margins. But you should know that McDonald's among other fast-food chains excels at cost management. In a somewhat realistic to conservative scenario, I assume the average variable cost per unit equals 25% of the average selling price. Compared to a single Big Mac, selling a value menu generates a 20% higher contribution margin in absolute terms. As a matter of fact, a value menu with a 15% discount pays off for McDonalds, as long as the percentage variable cost per unit does not exceed 50% of the selling price, which is an unrealistic scenario. In other words, McDonald's has nothing to lose in offering the Big Mac value menu. In the meantime, customers who trade up also benefit from the deal effect. So we have a win-win situation, in which everyone is happy.

I trust that you have seen those ordering kiosks in the McDonald's restaurants. Apart from reducing the need for customer-facing staff, they also contribute a great deal to facilitating bundling and cross-selling. Together with mobile ordering apps, the self-service kiosk could help the franchise rake back in nearly $2.7 billion in lost sales.[1] Wonder how it works? They make it much easier to order an enormously embarrassing amount and variety of food without the cashier or the customers waiting behind you looking at you!

But why did McDonald's and Co. take chicken wings off the value menus? Judging from the small sample of friends and family of mine, my best guess would be that chicken wings are so popular that they are a strong next candidate for becoming a hero product. Remember we just said that you usually do not need two hero products in a bundle? By including two heroes in bundle, you miss out on capturing the full pricing potential. Why? Because there are enough customers out there to buy a hero product at full price. This is exactly what my (poor) colleague and I did. We pay for what is indispensable for us, while we also keep falling for the deal effect, i.e., the discount of the value menu.

In addition to avoiding having two hero products in the bundle, it is crucial not to bundle the wrong items (pricing consultants refer to them as killers), which customers perceive to be inferior or of little value. To see why it is the case, let's take a look at an experiment that was included in the book *Thinking, Fast and Slow* by the Nobel laureate Daniel Kahneman. Although the book has had profound impact on behavioral pricing both in academia and in practice, there are only few instances where the word *price* itself is mentioned. Among these few exceptions is an experiment by Christopher Hsee, a leading scholar in behavioral science and marketing.

In the experiment, the respondents were tasked with pricing two sets of dinnerware, assuming that these are offered in a clearance sale in a local store. See the two sets in Fig. 1.

Two groups of respondents were shown only one of the sets. Guess which set had the higher price? Set A was priced at $23 on average while Set B at $33, i.e., there was nearly a 50% price difference! How did this happen? Set A and Set B contain the exact same dinner plates, soup/salad bowls and dessert plates in the same conditions, whereas Set A additionally has eight cups and eight saucers. Homo economicus should have valued Set A more and assigned

---

[1] https://www.businessinsider.com/mcdonalds-kiosk-vs-cashiers-photos-2018-3?r=DE&IR=T.

	Set A	Set B
Pieces in total	40	24
Dinner plates	8 pieces, all in good condition	
Soup/salad bowls	8 pieces, all in good condition	
Dessert plates	8 pieces, all in good condition	
Cups	8 pieces, 2 of them broken	
Saucers	8 pieces, 7 of them broken	

Fig. 1 Pricing experiment by Christopher Hsee. (Source: Kahneman, Daniel. Thinking, Fast and Slow. New York: Farrar, Straus And Giroux, 2011, reconstructed by the author)

a higher price to it. Yet we know that humans are genetically irrational, for better or worse. What matters most in the pricing experiment here is the average value of the dishes, which is much lower for Set A than for Set B due to the broken dishes. If the average value of a bundle dominates the value perception of a customer, it is not surprising that Set B is valued more. It is a principle known as *less is more*. In plain English, it means packing the right ones in a bundle is much more important than packing more items.

Although Kahneman himself is not even an economist, his work has had far-reaching influence on economics and management practice. He even won a Nobel Memorial Prize in Economic Sciences in 2002. The behavioral aspect of pricing has been gaining importance over the years, inspired by his work which actually barely mentions the word price. A solid understanding of what customers need and value does product managers a big favor in that they can be more confident about the prospect of the product when it is launched. Without this product launches are just like a lucky draw or being at the mercy of God. Product managers can do a better job, by factoring in customers' needs and their willingness to pay, early on in the research and development phase.

Smart microwave is one of my favorite examples that illustrate the importance of customer-centric thinking in product development. Microwaves are a great invention and a common household appliance. The use of this kitchen device is straightforward. On the front panel, there are two dials, which the user can turn to control time and power, respectively; it's as simple as that. The disadvantage of this kind of human-machine interface is obvious. The user needs to have product knowledge to grasp what time and power mean exactly for the heating outcome. The fact that different combinations of time and power may lead to the same outcome grants the user more flexibility but not necessarily more convenience. That very much needed product knowledge could be acquired through either reading through the user's manual or learning by doing. It is easy to tell that both solutions are tedious and sub-optimal from a consumers' point of view. If manufacturers realize this, shouldn't they try something smarter? Actually, many of them did try to be more user-friendly in that they pre-programmed recipes and created use-case-based buttons on the control panel on the front, such as warming up a glass of milk, boiling a glass of water, making a porridge, and unfreezing a piece of steak, and the list goes on. At first glance, one might think it is a great idea to link product function directly to customer needs. The users do not have to sweat over how to choose time and power any more.

Nevertheless, my personal experience shows that this is a well-meant solution that tends to fail. Years ago, I bought a smart microwave, as the salesperson convinced me of the embedded recipe functions as described above. And it happened to be on promotion. A couple of months went by, and I noticed that there were only two buttons on the control panel with visible fingerprints. The first one is the door switch, and the other is the quick start button for 30 seconds of heating. How come a wide range of options existed on this smart microwave that was supposed to make my life easier, while I ended up falling back into my old habits? In reflecting on my own behavior, I realized that I used the microwave primarily for fast cooking. The pre-programmed recipes actually had little to do with my cooking routine. It was also tedious to remember what all these buttons are meant for. As a matter of fact, it is a daunting task to exhaustively fit all recipes for all customer segments onto that limited space of the control panel without causing the user to be confused by these and to forego making any of the available choices in the end. All in all, maybe it is not such a great idea to bundle pre-defined cooking functions into microwaves. I came to realize why a relatively new microwave model would be promotion product in the first place.

Remember This!

- Bundling is a powerful tool to engage customers and generate extra profit, and it demonstrates that good pricing can lead to a win-win situation for both companies and consumers.
- Usually it is not a good idea to put two hero products in one bundle. Taking chicken wings out of value menu makes sense for McDonald's while irritating consumers.
- Avoid including killers (e.g., broken dishes) in the bundle.
- The right price for a bundle should be calculated, not guessed.
- Peter F. Drucker once said and I quote: "An innovation, to be effective, has to be simple and it has to be focused. It should do only thing, otherwise it confuses. If it is not simple, it won't work."

Grocery Box in Parts

What You Will Discover?

By now you have seen the tricks of bundling and why it makes sense for companies to offer bundles. At the root of a successful bundling act lies a good understanding of customer needs. If we follow the reasoning, what should companies do when their customers do not want the products to be grouped together? When does it make sense for companies to unbundle their offers?

IKEA is the master of offering many practical things at a reasonable price. Based on my observation, IKEA's wide range of products with a broad price spectrum results in a highly diversified customer base of people from all walks of life. We too have a great variety of items from IKEA in almost all rooms in our home. The IKEA stores offer a pleasant shopping experience complete with playgrounds for kids and restaurants for everyone, which rank tenth among the biggest fast-food chains in Germany.[1] No matter what, it is a good place to hang out for half a day, even without buying anything.

The other day Doreen and I went to visit an IKEA store near our apartment. While she was walking down the aisle looking for the items on her shopping list (we both have the old good habit of carrying a shopping list along, the best way to avoid impulsive shopping), an ad sign caught my attention (see Fig. 1).

---

[1] https://www.handelsblatt.com/unternehmen/handel-konsumgueter/systemgastronomie-das-sind-die-fast-food-champions-deutschlands/21048926.html?ticket=ST-389388-sPmzHvHIjIU GUAFlfqGE-ap4.

© Springer Nature Switzerland AG 2020

J. Y. Yang, *The Pricing Puzzle*, https://doi.org/10.1007/978-3-030-50777-0_6

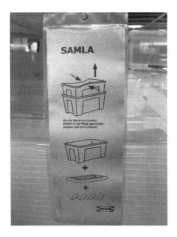

Fig. 1 Assembling instructions of a grocery box. (Source: author's own figure, picture taken in IKEA Godorf store on 23 May 2019)

€1.99/piece   €0.50/piece   €1.00/four pieces

€3.49/set

Fig. 2 Prices of the components of a grocery box. (Source: Author's own figure, picture taken in IKEA Godorf store on 23 May 2019)

It looked inconspicuous at first glance until you realized how the pricing was constructed. IKEA did not sell the complete Samla box as shown above as a whole set but instead sold it in pieces. See Fig. 2.

A Samla system (system is a big word for a box but a frequently used terminology in the IKEA world. I mean, why not be a bit ambitious?) comes in three parts: the box as the main component, the lid, and the clasps, which are stored separately in different places on the shelf. If you have bought furniture at IKEA before, you know that it is normal for components to be packaged and stored in different places in IKEA's pickup warehouse downstairs. In doing that, IKEA saves storage and logistics costs. But usually there is only one price for the whole set, unlike the Samla box shown above. Each part of the Salma system carries its own price tag: €1.99 for the box, €0.50 for the lid, and €1.00 for four clasps, which keep the lid locked to the box (a low-tech but effective solution). It is simple to work out with how much it will cost if you want it all: three parts for a total price of €3.49/set. It is still not that much money, yet a significantly higher sum than the box, or the "no-frills" version of the Samla system. There may be other considerations which I am not aware of. But the pricing as such was intriguing so that I took pictures (yeah, this is what a pricing consultant likes to do in his daily life).

What IKEA is doing here is unbundling. Previously, I have touched upon the concept the bundling and its benefits for both the seller and the buyer. Unbundling is the opposite strategy of bundling and can at times also be a winning strategy for all sides making the transaction. For example, unbundling could make sense in the following situations, namely, if:

1. Customer needs are diverse so that no bundled product can reasonably meet the needs of the majority. In other words, bundling decreases customers' value perception and deters them from making a purchase (as we saw from the dinnerware pricing experiment in the last story).
2. The bundled product appears to be too expensive or to exceed a critical psychological price threshold.
3. It is possible to break the bundle into distinct parts when the value of each is easy to comprehend, while the "no-frills" or the "naked" version is usable also as a stand-alone product.
4. There are customers who are willing to pay for add-ons in addition to the stand-alone product.

In the IKEA Samla case, the naked box looks like a bargain, costing only €1.99. From an assortment perspective, it serves as an attractive entry-level product: it satisfies the basic needs of the majority of customers to carry and put away stuff; the reasonably low price makes the purchase decision easier, as customers are usually less sensitive to low-priced products. For customers who want more, there is not only the lid to keep dust out and make stacking easier. But also there are also the clasps to make sure that the contents do not fall out accidentally. They can upgrade to having these benefits by paying just a bit more. From a behavioral pricing point of view, the price paid for the "naked" box is lowered. In other words, the purchases of the lid and the clasps are seen as add-ons, and are regarded as independent transactions, each of which only costs a little more money, bringing down the inhibitions to purchase them significantly. The outcome is a very good one for IKEA. Customers who want to have an entire Samla system will pay up to a whopping 75% premium compared to the "naked" version while still considering it a fair deal. No one forces them to buy it all.

The residential real estate industry provides us with another compelling example. When I first moved to Germany more than a decade ago, I marveled at the spacious corridors and open space in apartment buildings. The one feature that I like the most and do not find back in my hometown in Shanghai or anywhere else in China is that in Germany, every apartment gets a 3–5-ish square meter storage space in the basement. This is very practical, especially for families with kids and admittedly for hoarders. We moved house a couple of times over the years and always had a storage space in the basement. It is not surprising that I started to take it for granted that there is one in all residential buildings. However, reality has often proven me to be too naive in this respect.

In 2019, to fast-forward the story, we decided to move out of our rented apartment and get a house of our own, as the family had risen to five members and it is difficult to still fit into a decent apartment in a big city like Cologne. While browsing through the housing advertisements, I could not help noticing that many features I thought would be included in the price were singled out as special wish items. Typically, a basement and shower cabins are things no longer included in the base price. After checking with a few friends of ours, the no-frills housing model seemed to have become the new norm in Germany. Fully furnished houses are now dismantled into a base version with special items as add-ons. Both emotionally and financially, I disapprove of the unbundling approach as a potential house buyer, as you can imagine. But from a pricing consultant's point of view, this makes sense and kills two birds with one stone.

Firstly, unbundling makes the price look more attractive. The impact of this should not be underestimated. Nowadays almost all listings are online. Many people sort search results by price in ascending order. Lower prices therefore mean better positions in the search results, which in turn may lead to a better conversion rate. When people invest their time in investigating real estate offers, it is more difficult for them to move on even after they find out that it costs a lot more to build their dream home than the initial price tag suggests.

Secondly, it differentiates and makes the offer more palatable to potential buyers. The biggest risk of bundling arguably lies in including something (killers, if you remember from last story) that adversely affects customers' value perception. By unbundling, customers have the choice to not pay for things they do not need. The potential upside for the sellers is that they may be able to charge more, as customers expose their preference by selecting the special wish items. Such an exposure is an invitation for sellers to ask for a premium for these add-ons.

Serendipity continued when we went through the decoration plan with the real estate developer. The house was equipped with a so-called smart home system, which intelligently operates the electric devices inside the house, for example, the floor heating, the lighting, the window blinds, etc. You could also pre-program the ambient atmosphere so that the brightness or temperature adapts automatically to your needs. We were happy to learn that this was included in the base price. But there was a catch. The smart home system can be controlled by a panel mounted to the wall physically and by smartphone via an app remotely. Only the physical option was included in the base price. Bazinga! The app allows you to monitor the status of electric equipment at home in real time and adjust settings as you please. Everything nice comes with a price. Although the app is free to download, it will cost a few euros to use the app on a monthly basis! Subscription models are making inroads everywhere. In the end, we decided to spend more smartly and live less smartly.

There are many more examples of unbundling around us: the low-cost airlines that charge all kinds of possible surcharges, the equipment packages of passenger cars, and the collecting of football player cards, just to name a few. Bundling or unbundling? There is no unambiguous answer to this question, because it is not the right question to ask. The right, underlying question should rather be: how can I better identify and satisfy the customers' needs? The right price is the trophy given for the right answer.

Remember This!

- There is no right or wrong about bundling or unbundling. The decisive factor is how consumers perceive it and pay for it.
- Unbundling makes sense especially when the main product covers the basic need, while there are customer groups out there to pay extra for add-ons that suit their use cases.
- As a consumer, you should resist the temptation of buying all the add-ons, as you probably have a finite budget. Spend smartly and focus on what really matters to you. This happens also to be what I tell my sons whenever they want yet another new toy.

Random Thoughts Up in the Air

What You Will Discover?

Airlines are notoriously troubled with their finances, and many of them have been trying to save money on in-flight catering in an effort to keep up profitability, even prior to the COVID-19 crisis. The deterioration of catering services is profound; it is after all an integral part of the flight experience. Isn't there a better alternative to achieve cost reduction?

I am writing this piece on a 12-h flight from Shanghai to Frankfurt, my most frequently travelled long-haul route. It seems to be the right topic for the right place. The award-winning movie *Up in the air* was released exactly 10 years ago and is one of my all-time favorites. The movie, which unfolds around a corporate downsizer and frequent flyer (played by *George Clooney*), has left a profound impact on the development of my personal travel rituals. Scenes involving packing for travel and navigating airports rub off on me. Whenever I arrive at the airport, my airport instinct will kick in automatically like there is a built-in navigator inside me. For example, I would move much faster at the airport than outside of it. In part this is because of my luggage kickboard (highly recommendable travel kit!); I am usually the first one to roll to the luggage claim area after landing.

Whenever I take a day-time long-haul flight like the one from Shanghai to Frankfurt, I like to take the advantage of not being connected to the internet in order to thus get some work done, which requires slow thinking. I have mixed feeling about almost all major airlines having recently started to offer Wi-Fi connections on their long-haul flights. More often than not, the

© Springer Nature Switzerland AG 2020
J. Y. Yang, *The Pricing Puzzle*, https://doi.org/10.1007/978-3-030-50777-0_7

connection is rationed, and even if you secure a log-in, it drops off all the time which causes more anxiety than that it gives convenience.

In recent years I have developed a travel habit of not eating any food on flights, especially on long-haul flights. It buys me more time for work or (even) leisure during the flight. I am used to landing hungry. I also came to realize that abstinence on board helps me get over jet lags after landing more quickly. I just need to stay hydrated. To that end, the airlines are really doing a good job at making things easier for me. The food is just horrible and getting worse across classes and airlines, based on my own experience which is also echoed by many of my friends and colleagues.

It is common knowledge that airlines suck at making money, ironically the big ones in particular. Take the United States as an example: Bankruptcies have become a way of life for the legacy carriers including the big three—American Airlines, United Airlines, and Delta Air Lines.[1] As a matter of fact, the profitability of the aviation industry across the board has fluctuated greatly over the years.

The traditional full-service airlines, in particular, are in a catch-22 situation. On the one hand, they have to live up to the expectation of providing comprehensive service to all passengers, not only up in the air but also on the ground. On the other hand, they are struggling to adapt to intensifying competition and having to find ways to keep their costs under control. As petty as it may appear, every cent on the bottom line counts. Food service is at the top of the cost-cutting list, as it has little to with the most important mission that passenger airlines are supposed to fulfill—moving people from one place to another.

Onboard food service used to be given a more important role if we look at the history of passenger aviation. On 11 October 1919, a remodeled airplane that had a capacity of merely a dozen people departed from London to Paris. As the flight time was around noon, lunch boxes that contained sandwiches and some fruit were on sale for 3 shillings apiece on board. That was the first-ever in-flight meal on record, exactly a hundred years ago.[2]

Since then, in-flight meals have become an integral part of the flight experience. In the early days of civil aviation, when commercial flights were still a rarity, the airlines went to great lengths to spoil passengers with lavish food and beverage delights. This was also the case in China. In the early years after the introduction of a reform and opening policy, the supply of premium food

---

[1] https://www.investopedia.com/stock-analysis/031714/why-airlines-arent-profitable-dal-ual-aal-luv-jblu.aspx.
[2] https://www.huxiu.com/article/319231.html.

and beverages was very restricted, though airlines were able to provide highly sought-after items such as *Maotai Baijiu* (arguably the best Chinese liquor) and *Chunghwa* cigarettes in flight. I was then too young to have had experience. But it was exotic enough to imagine passengers being able to drink high-grade baijiu and smoking cigarettes on the plane.

Suddenly, the cabin light was turned on, taking my attention away from the laptop screen. A female voice started to speak over the cabin broadcast. It was lunch time. While the stewardess was about to introduce the choices we would be able to make for main dishes, I thought to myself: *"Will it be beef rice, fish noodle or pork rice?"* The female voice went on: *"We will be serving beef rice and fish noodle today. Either kind of dishes is limited in numbers …"* Bingo. I was glad that I had eaten something proper before the departure.

As a matter of fact, the old good days of in-flight delicacies are long gone with the wind. The airlines are turning every stone around to maintain profitability. Without doubt, airlines' biggest cost block is fuel, which typically accounts for about 25% of total operating costs. Other cost items include airport take-off and landing fees, depreciation of aircraft and parts, and staff remuneration, which collectively represent about 50% of operating cost. The catering service makes up just about 4% of total cost.[3] However, oil prices, depreciation, take-off and landing fees, etc. cannot be fully controlled by airlines. While in-flight meals only represent a small portion of the costs, airlines enjoy broad discretion in cost-saving measures involving food and drinks.

In 2018, profit per passenger for the three biggest Chinese airlines—Air China, China Eastern, and China Southern—was approximately 67, 23, and 21 RMB. In the meantime, they were estimated to be spending between 24 and 34 RMB per passenger on in-flight catering.[4] Take China Southern as an example. If we make a conservative assumption that the average spend on in-flight catering is 24 RMB, this is already more than it earns per passenger. If the airline could cut the catering cost by 20%, profit would be improved by more than 20%. Not just for China Southern, I believe the degree of deterioration in both food quality and quantity that I have witnessed in the recent years must go way beyond 20%. Previously, I was also amused to read articles that defended the necessity of airlines to downsize in-flight catering service out of safety reasons.

The horrid catering service onboard made me rethink my belief that differentiation is a superior strategy compared to a low-cost strategy. When you differentiate, you have more control over your own fate. No one can prevent

---

[3] http://frcc.chinabaogao.com/jiaotong/201804/04263330422018.html.
[4] https://www.huxiu.com/article/319231.html.

you from innovating and coming up with something new. There will always be something new that appeals to your existing and/or prospective customers. However, if you decide to go down the road of a low-cost strategy, you are at the mercy of the competition. There will always be competitors with deeper pockets or those crazy enough to buy market shares at any cost. When it gets out of hand, negative prices are also seen to fuel competition for customers, i.e., customers are being paid to use the products or services in question. As crazy as it sounds, this did happen, e.g., in the bicycle sharing market in China.

The full-service airlines are supposed to have more cards to play, to differentiate the offers, and to exploit willingness to pay of different segments. Culinary experience could have constituted an instrumental differentiator from their peers and low-cost carriers. But now the big airlines are acting in concert to cut down spending on in-flight meals to keep the bottom line in the black zone. I believe that they are short-sighted and are turning the wrong stone. The practice reminds me of notorious tricks such as reducing the size of sparkling water bottles, enlarging the hole of the opening of a the toothpaste tube, and the like. In case you have not noticed, chewing gums have been hideously downsized so that now you need two instead of one as a standard dose. Leading brands even ran advertising campaigns to educate consumers that chewing two gums is the way to go.

Cliché has it that low-cost carriers are successful because they let go of all cost-generating services in favor of cheaper air tickets and to compensate for the lost opportunities in charging outrageous prices for first class and business class seats. In my view, it is only partially true. Low-cost carriers also differentiate, just in a different way compared to full-range airlines. If you have flown with a low-cost airline, you may have noticed that low carriers are stricter with luggage amounts permitted and tend to have less service staff on the ground and less catering offerings (and not for free!) up in the air. It is obvious that the comfort part in air traveling is very limited with low-cost carriers. From a pricing standpoint, the low-cost carriers spare no effort to seize every opportunity to increase the total amount of tickets with frills, of which individuals have different value perceptions and, in turn, different degrees of willingness to pay. If you want to carry an additional piece of luggage, you will pay a luggage surcharge. Moreover, some low-cost carriers will charge even more for an ad hoc luggage check-in, if you have not booked it in advance.

The approach brings two benefits with it. Firstly, customers are encouraged to be more mindful of carrying only what is essential on the journey. Flight costs are mainly driven by cargo and passenger weight. So it is effectively a cost reduction measure; secondly, for those who do have to travel with bulky luggage, it feels less painful when the luggage surcharge is separated from the air ticket. Recently, we have also been seeing low-cost airlines setting up a business class-like section, where passengers will have larger leg room and better catering service included. The boundaries between low-cost and full-range airlines are become more and more blurred, with the former increasingly offering differentiated value-adding services, the latter failing to provide meaningful differentiation, let alone any monetization from these.

The changing dynamic between low-cost and full-range airlines is reflected on the bottom line. In the United States, the pioneering low-cost carrier Southwest enjoys the highest profit margin (16.5%), belittling the traditional large carriers. The average profit margin across those seven biggest US airlines is 9%.[5] As a matter of fact, the low-cost carriers such as Southwest Airlines and JetBlue even beat the legacy airlines in revenue, making it to be among the Top 5 carriers in the United States.[6] It is a similar situation in China. The most profitable carrier in China is Spring Airlines, a low-cost carrier with a net profit margin of 11.5%. The aforementioned Big Three have an average return on sales of 3%.[7]

Saving money on food and beverages is a kind of salami slicing tactic used by financially troubled airlines. As said earlier, it would have an immediate big impact on the bottom line, as the baseline is very low. Nevertheless, the absolute upside potential is also limited. In the meantime, I think the long-term side effect on customer experience tends to get under-estimated. The culprit behind this is cost-oriented thinking. If the focus lies on reducing the cost, there is a maximum of 4% return on sales at play. If the airlines regard in-flight catering service a topline opportunity, the sky is the limit. Ironically, sky is the airlines' home turf.

I just wonder how come the airlines spend so much money on the dynamic pricing of the tickets while ignoring the chance to differentiate in-flight catering offerings. It would be cool to order a food and beverage package in the app in advance. It would go so far beyond the scope of this book to investigate how the airlines' apps could improve their functionality user-friendliness that I hereby curb my enthusiasm to elaborate. In a nutshell, I could imagine a good-better-best type of pricing bundle would fit very well. The passengers would also be happy to take the offer, after what they have suffered in recent years. After all, there is always a silver lining.

---

[5] https://money.com/airline-profit-per-passenger/.
[6] https://www.investopedia.com/stock-analysis/031714/why-airlines-arent-profitable-dal-ual-aal-luv-jblu.aspx.
[7] http://www.hnhtyxgs.com/hkjj/_A__3572.htm.

p.s. I looked but did not find reliable statistics on how much airplane food goes to waste. My guess is that it is a lot. It is a shame that so much food is wasted while there are still people starving. Taking food out of standard offers on the flight is probably also best from a sustainability point of view. No one ever starves on the flight. Hedonists or people in need can still pre-order and pay for the food.

Remember This!

- Airlines are too cost-oriented to overlook the profit potential from providing better, differentiated catering service on board.
- The long-term side effect of an inferior catering service tends to be underestimated.
- Airlines would be better off by providing more individual catering offers (unlimited topline potential) instead of cutting spending on food and beverages across the board (limited impact).
- Abstinence on board helps getting over jet lag sooner!

Carpe Diem

What You Will Discover?

It is no secret that cinema operators are dependent on sales of popcorn and other merchandise to stay profitable. Nevertheless, the diverging pricing trend of the main product, i.e., the movie ticket (being commoditized), and the ancillary product, e.g., popcorn (being premiumized), in China in the last decade is remarkable. Behind the scenes is the rising importance of an experience economy, as younger generations are increasingly living in the moment. What does the new consumerism that is rich in experience bode for pricing strategy?

I have been telling my younger single friends: Do not dread marriage. Wedlock is not going to change your life as much as you might think. It is just one more person to spend time with under the same roof. You still get to do what you want to do most of the time, provided that you have made the right decision choosing a spouse. However, things may change drastically once you have kids. The point of gravity of life then shifts considerably. The little one(s) will change your lifestyle and your attitude toward life forever. You will be obliged to give up some of the mundane pleasures that you used to have— dining out, hanging out with friends at short notice, or going to movies. Since our eldest son was born, Doreen and I have rarely had any opportunity to go to the cinema on our own. If my memory is correct, we have not seen a single movie together in almost 7 years and counting.

Last summer we took the kids back to Shanghai on vacation. One day Doreen took our eldest boy to see a popular cartoon movie. I was supposed to meet up with them after the movie at the cinema. I arrived a bit early. The movie had not ended yet. Having not been in a cinema for a long time, I could not help looking around in the foyer. There were few people standing in front of the box office. Almost everything in the consumer service that can be digitalized has been largely digitalized in China. This is also the case with movies. Before going to the cinema, people check movie reviews, purchase movie tickets, and even select seats in various online channels or apps. Admission to the cinema is also made easy. Moviegoers just need a QR-code on their smartphones which can then be used as an electronic ticket.

There was this electric easel board standing right in front of the box office, which showed the prices of the newly released movie that happened to be what Doreen and our son were watching (see Fig. 1).

There are three different seat categories, these are shown vertically. Per category there are four possible sales channels which are shown horizontally. In the normal seat category (the first row), the price difference between the most expensive and the cheapest tickets was 50%. The cheapest ticket was only available to the cinema's club members. In general, the cinema operators are very reliant on third-party ticketing platforms to generate traffic. The commission fee for a ticket purchased usually lies in the range of 5–10%, not

Fig. 1 Movie ticket prices by channel. (Source: Author's own figure, picture taken in Shanghai in the summer of 2019)

including additional fees that may arise for value-adding services. But the cinema operator here was undercutting its channel partners by 50%. It really craves to foster its own *private traffic*. Private traffic is a trending concept in influencer marketing in China. Public traffic comes from dominant online marketplaces, where merchants have to fight hard to get the attention of customers. Amazon and Tmall are well-known general marketplaces, which have a broad product assortment. There are also specialized platforms catering to the specific needs of individual consumers, such as apartment rental, food delivery, travel agencies, and movies, just to name a few. The rules of the game are similar, resulting in an increasing importance of platforms which have full control of the traffic, and by that over the customers of the merchants. As the marketplaces get more and more crowded, it also becomes increasingly more costly to acquire and retain attention. In contrast, private traffic is private to merchants and enables long-lasting bonding with their customers. The most common forms of private traffic are customer loyalty programs, memberships, fan communities, etc., through which the merchants have essential information about the customers.

While my mind wandered, my eyes caught sight of something else that was interesting: The movie ticket could be bought for about 20 RMB, i.e., less than 3 EUR. When I used to buy movie tickets more often in the old days, i.e., probably more than 10 years ago, a movie ticket costs typically 50 RMB or more in Shanghai. What a deflation! Considering China's CPI (consumer price index) in the last decade, the price should be at least 20% higher than 10 years ago.

Online video streaming services as well as other available forms of entertainment pose a severe threat to the cinema industry. It is not uncommon these days to see only a few seats filled at a movie. Full houses are privileges that seem reserved only for blockbuster movies. With deteriorating turnout, cinema operators find themselves struggling with making a profit. How can they make both ends meet with such low ticket prices?

There was a snack bar in the prime location of the cinema foyer, radiating a tempting smell of sweets, salt, and butter; popcorn! The food and beverage menu was not long. So it was not difficult to figure out that popcorn was only available in combination with a soft drink of choice. The menu price started from 33 RMB, i.e., it was by 65% more expensive than the cheapest movie ticket. I knew that popcorn is essential to the economic health of cinemas, but the steep popcorn price compared to the ticket price was still shocking for someone that had not set his foot in a cinema in years. The movie was over. Doreen and our kid came out of the movie hall. Naturally, I asked her what price she had paid, pointing at the prices on the electric easel board. Doreen rolled her eyes at me, as if I were challenging her price-savviness. Okay, I was a bit out of touch with reality.

Later on, out of curiosity, I downloaded a movie booking app to check the prices of movie tickets and snacks (yes, the universal app provides details on pricing on everything about mainstream cinemas across the country). I spot-checked five cinemas in Shanghai to confirm the pattern I saw at the cinema: movie tickets were sharply discounted across the board; popcorn was exclusively available in bundles. The cinema operators seemed desperate to make extra money outside of the ticket box. It could also explain why the cinema operators were eager to have their private traffic. Third-party ticketing platforms took a sizeable cut of the revenue of food and beverage pre-ordered online.

The combination of low-priced movie ticket and high-priced popcorn comprises a two-dimensional price structure, which is a proven approach to exploiting the willingness to pay in heterogeneous customer segments. In the cinema example, the movie ticket is the base product and the popcorn among other snacks the value-added service. The high price positioning of popcorn effectively distinguishes customer segments. On the one hand, the cinemas need to attract as many moviegoers as possible in the face of intensifying competition; on the other hand, they also have to be wary of the profitability of the incoming visits. Cinema operators resort to high-margin products such as snacks and beverages to monetize the traffic into the cinema.

The drastic increase in the popcorn price, as well as the creativity shown in creating a variety of snacks and beverages offerings in the last decade, showcases, on the one hand, the pressing need for cinemas to tap into additional revenue sources to compensate for declining ticket box revenue. On the other hand, it also takes advantage of consumers' behavioral psychology, namely, "*I have saved money on the movie ticket. I deserve a popcorn treat.*" Customers will lower their guard for purchases, once they set foot on the premises of the cinema. For people who crave the entire experience package, the popcorn is almost imperative. They will have a much higher willingness to pay, which spills over to food and beverage, and even some other merchandise.

It is worth noting that the millennials or their younger generations are placing more importance on experience. People used to buy and own stuff; youngsters today like to spend in order to experience something. Ownership is old-fashioned. Experience is the new consumerism. Eating popcorn completes the movie watching experience. If there is a reason to believe that a significant part of the population values the ritualistic experience, it makes perfect sense for cinema operators to subsidize movies tickets to enlarge the customer base and earn money from things that complete and enrich the experience including but not limited to popcorn. The competition should be thus centering on providing the best overall movie-watching experience. Whoever wins the loyalty of customers will have a better chance to survive and thrive in the long run.

Cinema operators could learn from German railway's loyalty program BahnCard. The passengers need to pay hundreds of euros in advance for a BahnCard annually, which means rail card in English. The BahnCard holder is entitled to a 25–100% discount on the train tickets for a year, depending on which card is bought.

The BahnCard makes sense for frequent travelers wanting to optimize railway expenses, if and only if they have a good idea about how much they are going to travel in the next 12 months. Take BahnCard 50 (which grants the holder a 50% discount) as an example (see Fig. 2). After having paid €515 for the loyalty card, she or he gets a 50% discount off the regular train fare. Only after the total mileage traveled exceeds approximately 2000 km will the BahnCard 50 start to pay off for the card holder. In reality, people tend to overestimate their usage. Consequently, a passenger that may be totally fine with a BahnCard 25 (which grants 25% discount) might wrongly (or not?) buy a BahnCard 50 instead. The seemingly irrational behavior can be rationally explained by people being willing to pay extra in exchange for "*peace of mind*"—*I know I might not travel so much to break even with purchase of a BahnCard 50. But I am going to buy it because I do not want to feel I ought to have bought a BahnCard 50 that after having travelled too much.*

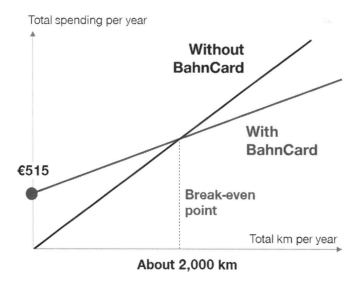

Fig. 2 Total railway spending with/without BahnCard—first class. (Source: Author's own figure; BahnCard price er February 2020)

According to Simon-Kucher's analysis, the average BahnCard holder does indeed pay to play it safe. We observe that BahnCard 50 holders as a whole are actually enjoying only about a 30% discount instead of the 50% discount which they expected. Every time I go through the BahnCard example, I marvel at this simple yet powerful pricing construct. How come it is not implemented in more industries?

Last summer while we were with the kids in China, we also spent a few days in Hangzhou, where Doreen and Alibaba's Jack Ma come from. During our stay there, I took our eldest son to the Municipal Natural History Museum on a scorching hot day. As we finished the visit early, we decided to then go by the bookstore next to it to kill some time. As it was summer vacation time, the place was packed with parents and kids. After wandering around the book shelves for a while, we got ourselves a couple of comic books and decided to have some refreshments. There was a coffee shop inside the bookstore. But all of the tables were fully occupied. The customers were largely moms and kids, showing no sign to leave any time soon. So we had to sit in the open air under the sun. After having found a seat at for my son, I went back to the bar to fetch us some drinks. And I saw this (Fig. 3):

Wow. It is an interesting beverage assortment with exotic prices, considering the mundane environment of the bookstore. The cheapest drink is a small bottle of Evian spring water, which costs 20 RMB, i.e., almost 3 USD. You should know that books in China are extremely cheap by Western standards. For a similar book, the German version retails for about 50 Euro; the Chinese copy will likely be available for less than 30 RMB. I sucked it up and bought

Fig. 3 Coffee bar in a book store. (Source: Author's own figure, taken in Hangzhou in high summer of 2019)

two bottles of Perrier in the end, which cost 5 RMB more than Evian. I mean, why not? I did not have to pay much for the books, after all. Let's go the whole hog.

Wait … I suddenly experienced a Déjà vu. Bookstores are no different than cinemas! A bookstore nowadays no longer makes money by selling books. Instead, books are becoming a customer traffic driver. Consumers are shifting their budget to buy the frills that make a bookstore visit a pleasant experience. I surmise that charging for an experience is a superior price model, wherever possible. The pleasure of owning something passes quickly. Experience is memorable and personal. As such, the money paid for an experience is well spent.

> **Remember This!**
>
> - Merchants are fighting hard to reduce dependence on third-party platforms by converting public traffic into private traffic which is private to merchants and enables the establishment of long-lasting bonds with their customers.
> - A two-dimensional price structure is conducive to expanding the customer base as well as generating a higher willingness to pay among certain customer groups.
> - Consumers have a high willingness to pay for an experience, as an experience is memorable and personal.
> - Carpe diem, and be ready to pay/charge for it.

The Tale of the Midnight Diner

What You Will Discover?

Customer loyalty is rather a rarity in our time. Nonetheless, retailers attach great importance to building and maintaining customer loyalty. At the end of the day, it comes down to maximizing customer lifetime value. We observe a plethora of loyalty programs around us, many of which are ill-designed. Why is that? The tale of the midnight diner provides a simple yet telling case when viewed as an example of the pitfalls of a loyalty program.

Self-control is one of my strengths. For example, I am disciplined with my diet in order to stay fit and look sharp, avoiding carbohydrates and sugar as much as possible. Occasionally, I switch into hedonist mode and get myself something tasty but not necessarily good for my health.

Lanzhou-style hand-pulled beef noodle (*lamian* in Chinese) is my all-time favorite treat. According to my knowledge, *lamian* is unique to China. What is special about it is that the noodle is twisted, pulled, and stretched from a dough with hand, using the weight of the dough without using any other tool. The quality of the noodle hinges on the craftsmanship of the noodle master, who typically undergoes years of hard training and practice. Google *lamian,* should you be interested in the culinary details.

These days it is not easy to find a good noodle place. And amusingly, most Lanzhou *lamian*-eating places in China are seldom run by people from Lanzhou or the province Gansu which it belongs to. Many of the owners and lamian masters are most likely from Henan Province, where the iPhones are assembled.

© Springer Nature Switzerland AG 2020

J. Y. Yang, *The Pricing Puzzle*, https://doi.org/10.1007/978-3-030-50777-0_9

There is a midnight diner near my apartment in Shanghai, which specializes in hand-pulled beef noodle. Despite being mundane and crowded most of the time, it is my favorite noodle place in town. It is my go-to place, when I crave a quick bite late at night. Although I like to call it midnight diner, it is actually open for business around the clock. There is a popular Japanese drama TV series called *Midnight Diner*, or *Shinya Shokudo* in Japanese. It depicts ordinary patrons who have a moment of peace and relief from their busy life while having simple food prepared by the master in a diner that opens at midnight. The lamian place reminds me of *Shinya Shokudo*, whenever I sit in the diner surrounded by people from all walks of life.

As I sometimes pass by the diner during normal working hours, I can tell the place is popular among people working or living in the vicinity during lunch and dinner time. But the noodles there really beat everything else. The diner has been around for over 10 years and has maintained its quality standard. It is a great achievement for a mom-and-pop business.

The other night, I went out for my midnight treat after finishing off the daily hustle. I noticed a big poster stand outside the diner, which said 20% discount straight on any purchase in celebration of the 13th anniversary of the diner. I did not recall it did such a campaign at its tenth anniversary, which would be more worthwhile to celebrate, or on any other occasions in the recent past. Out of curiosity, I had a brief chat with the owner while ordering and paying at the counter. In his own account, he felt like rewarding the loyal customers. It was a very nice gesture. I myself also appreciated the 20% discount on the bill.

The noodle was as delicious as usual and then my pricing consultant instinct kicked in. I asked myself the following questions:

- Are direct discounts the best way to reward customers?
- Is there a better way to communicate the discounts?
- Does it pay off for the owner?

It has become an increasingly common practice for retailers and restaurants to offer special prices or discount to celebrate anniversaries. From a customer perspective, it will be appreciated, for a moment at least. Who does not like experiencing a windfall? It increases one's well-being. It is human to like treats. The tricky part of the story is that it is also human to discount the value of something that is sold at a discount, especially when the discounting is recurring and expected. Although anniversary discounts are a nice thing to do, customers tend to take them for granted.

Discounts are ubiquitous in today's retail landscape across the world. In the meanwhile, retailers are struggling with their discount strategy, as the volume-boosting effect of discount has been waning, as everyone else is also offering some sort of discounts. Over time, it has become a self-fulfilling prophecy. The very act of granting discounts openly has led to customers feeling justified in getting them and has reinforced their wish to get even higher discounts. There is no easy way out. It is hard for retailers to deviate from such me-too practice. As a result, consumers often come across "*moon prices,*" by means of which retailers create the impression of offering attractive deals by first raising list prices. I find undifferentiated discounts are especially detrimental to business. No one wants to be treated as being an average. If you want to do it right, understanding what matters to your customers is imperative.

Ubiquitous discounts are putting mounting pressure on the margins of the retailers, which are either tempted or forced to inflate recommended retail prices in anticipation of discounts and squeeze their suppliers to reduce purchase cost in an effort to protect their margins. Some others are also trying to develop smarter discounting approaches, where differentiation is the key.

UNIQLO serves as a good example. The Japanese apparel brand offers discounts in a selective way. For one thing, it rarely grants discounts across the board. It runs promotion selectively on those items that are most likely to drive traffic into stores and eventually boost the sales of other items. For another, it usually does this within a limited time window, effectively planting a sense of scarcity among its customers. Moreover, it has a consistent pricing strategy for online and offline channels so that the customers can be assured that they have the best price no matter where the purchase takes place.

To get back to the loyalty campaign, or whatever it was that the diner owner was staging, I believe that it was ill-designed albeit well-intended. Actually, being a long-time customer, I empathize with the diner owner, a good guy indeed. I understand that it is his way of saying thank you to his loyal customers. But the way he does it is by wasting money. It probably won't entice existing customers to come to the diner more often or buy more in the future. There won't be any new customers acquired through the campaign, as the customer traffic in the vicinity of the diner is more or less static. Even if there are, the incremental revenue will be limited due to capacity constraints. The anniversary discounts are like transient fireworks. A loyal customers' joy is short-lived, if there is any, while the long-term pay-off is most likely uncertain.

In the meantime, the short-term financial damage is real and direct. The math is straightforward. I estimate the gross margin of a noodle soup to be around 50%. Deducting all miscellaneous operating expenses, the diner will probably end up with an operating margin between 10 and 20% at best, depending on how the sales turnover develops throughout the year. No matter what, the odds are that a 20% discount threatens to wipe out all profit in one go.

One might argue that this is not the full picture. What about cross-selling, i.e., the incremental sales opportunities? Indeed, it deserves the benefit of the doubt. But remember the discounts are granted for the entire menu. That is exactly what makes it so detrimental. Except for the high-margin products such as alcoholic beverages, the additional sales opportunities are profit destroyers in disguise and would just deepen the wound. In comparison to apparel retailers and other businesses, budget restaurants or diners are much less sophisticated/privileged in portfolio pricing to be able to assign different roles (e.g., traffic driver vs. profit driver) to different product groups.

Another small yet important design flaw lies in the communication of the discounts. While UNIQLO sets clear expectation on the time horizon of the discounts, our diner owner was being ambiguous about the duration of his campaign. I guess, either he overlooked it, or he thought it was not important enough to be mentioned, or he was indecisive about how long the campaign should run and wanted to postpone the decision until he was sure. In my view, this was a miscalculation. The most crucial part of managing customer loyalty is managing expectation. In other words, it is important to set the bar a bit lower for expectations of having a positive surprise. Customers are only satisfied when you exceed their expectation. In essence, customer satisfaction is relative. As the duration was not communicated— and of course we all knew it would end sometime in the foreseeable future— customers who then come into the diner only to find that the discounts have been taken back would because of that have an unpleasant moment of insight. When a bad thing is certain to happen, it is better to break the news ahead of time.

A few days later, I went by the diner to find the poster was removed secretively just like how it appeared in the first place. I sighed and walked in. At that moment, I wished I could have come over more often, while the 20%

Fig. 1 Hand-pulled beef noodle (*lamian*). (Source: author's own figure, picture taken in Shanghai in the summer of 2019)

discount was still in place. But what mattered most is that the lamian was as good as always. See Fig. 1 for impression of the delicious lamian.

Remember This!

- Customer loyalty cannot be taken for guaranteed in our time. Businesses need to go to great lengths to ensure customer loyalty.
- Many loyalty programs are ill-designed, leaving money on the table without it having real impact.
- Managing customer loyalty is about managing expectation—customers are only satisfied when they experience what exceeds their expectation.

The Burden of Fame

What You Will Discover?

Promotions at grocery stores have become a recurring business. Retailers rotate popular brands during a promotion and usually offer very attractive discounts. A discount of 50% or higher is not uncommon. Why do retailers go to such greats lengths? Have you ever noticed what kind of brands retailers usually put on promotion campaigns?

Italian kitchen is beloved across Europe and goes way beyond the continent, inspiring culinary delights and discoveries around the world. Among all these, Italian pasta is that which is most popular. Spaghetti Bolognese is a safe choice for adults as well as kids. I can say, from my own experience, that grocery stores and supermarkets across Germany keep a large variety of pasta with a rich variety of brands and types.

Take REWE as an example, which is the second largest grocery supermarket chain and a leading high-end retail brand in Germany. Search for keyword *pasta* in its online shop resulted in over 400 SKUs (stock keeping units) in 11 pages. Impression of the first page of the search results is shown in Fig. 1 as follows.

Of all packaged pasta, Barilla is the best pasta brand I know of and my default choice. You can tell it is popular from the fact that Barilla's classic blue paper package occupies the first row on the first page of search results shown above. As a matter of fact, the unique blue paper package also makes Barilla easily stand out on the crowded pasta shelves in the brick-and-mortar stores of the supermarkets. Although it is not necessarily the most expensive pasta

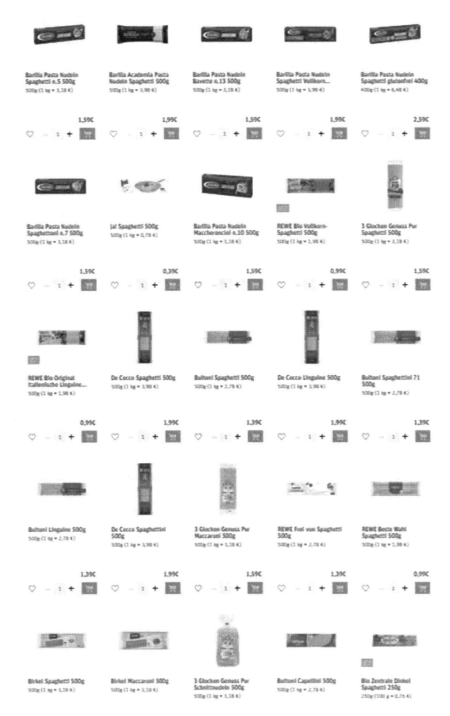

Fig. 1 Search results of pasta on REWE online store. (Source: https://shop.rewe.de/productList?search=pasta, 1st July 2019)

brand, Barilla is in the league of premium pasta brands. The presentation and the quality of the product justify this.

REWE launched several lines of premium gourmet products bearing the brand name *REWE Beste Wahl* (meaning REWE Best Choice in English) a few years ago. Pasta is also among the REWE-branded product categories. In most cases, Beste Wahl is positioned on par with or slightly lower than established brands. However, for the same type of pasta, Barilla sells for €3.18 per kg, REWE Beste Wahl costs €1.98 per kg. The former is 61% more expensive than the latter, which again suggests that Barilla is a high-end pasta brand. See Fig. 2.

But there is a catch. On the exact day of 1 July 2019, there was a promotion going on both online and offline. The entire assortment of Barilla pasta was sold at less than half the regular price, undercutting the price of REWE Beste Wahl. See Fig. 3 below.

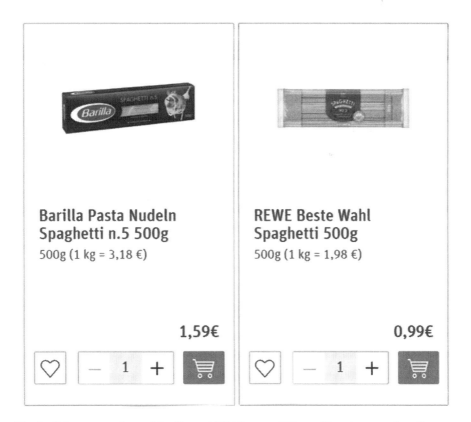

Fig. 2 Price comparison of Barilla and REWE pasta 500 g, without promotion. (Source: https://shop.rewe.de/productList?search=pasta, 24th June 2019)

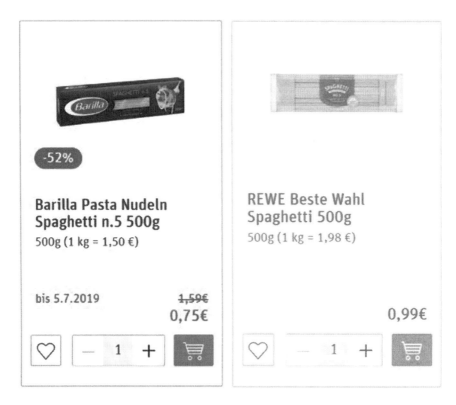

Fig. 3 Price comparison of Barilla and REWE pasta 500 g, with promotion. (Source: https://shop.rewe.de/productList?search=pasta, 1st July 2019)

Even though I am not the one in our household who usually does the most pantry shopping, I have a vivid memory of the nearby REWE store putting Barilla on promotion on a regular basis in the more than years which I spent in Cologne. The promotion flyers in the mailbox as well as posters in the supermarket facilities often feature Barilla on sale with deep, often very deep discounts. It defies common sense that high-end brands usually do not engage in promotions, let alone in massive, clearance-like promotions. To be on the safe side, I asked my wife Doreen, who is in charge of finance and purchasing in our household, about the matter. She confirmed that Barilla regularly appears on promotions. It turns out that she has accustomed herself to not buy Barilla unless it is on promotion. When there is a promotion, which usually runs for a week, she tends to hoard to the extent that there is enough of it for us to eat till the next round of promotion comes up. As far as I can recall, we seldom run out of stock of Barilla at home. One can imagine that this buying behavior is definitely detrimental for a premium brand like Barilla. The retailer REWE seemingly has also little to gain from a prolonged, regular promotion, as it has taught consumers two things:

- It can be expected that Barilla goes on sale on a regular basis.
- It is smart to buy Barilla in bulk when it is on sale.

So why would REWE do such a thing to foster undesired behavior of consumers? Before I get to this question, let me share two more personal observations in REWE supermarkets.

Firstly, apart from pasta, a product category that is also regularly discounted is ground coffee. Germans love drinking coffee, even more than beer. An average German drinks 100 liters of beer in a year, while consuming 150 liters of coffee annually,[1] i.e., 1.4 cups of coffee on a daily basis.[2] At REWE, the choice of coffee brands is less abundant than that of pasta. Promotions usually take turns across different brands.

Secondly, despite the fact that REWE carries a large assortment of pasta brands in its assortment, other brands rarely appear on promotion, if ever. It seems that Barilla is the designated brand for pasta promotion, for better or worse.

Now coming back to the question of why REWE has chosen to heavily discount Barilla on a recurring basis, my hypothesis is that REWE deliberately uses Barilla as a loss leader (items sold with heavy discounts, meaning a negative gross margin at times) in an effort to lure consumers into the store in the hope of earning money on the other items that they might add to their shopping baskets while shopping (pantry-loading) pasta. Unlike coffee, in which category there is no clear champion brand, in my humble opinion, Barilla is the overall preferred brand in the pasta category so that it is safe to assume that it will resonate with the vast majority of customers. Being a high-value brand, Barilla has a high price anchor in consumers' minds. A high percentage discount on high-value brands such as Barilla should be extremely appealing to consumers. From the vantage point of both consumers and retailers, it makes perfect sense to put Barilla on promotion. It is obvious that the key to this strategy's success is that consumers will actually also buy other higher margin products after they have bought what they came into the store for.

---

[1] https://www.statista.com/statistics/540025/beer-consumption-per-capita-in-germany/.

[2] https://www.coffeeteacy.com/blog/post/30236/Germany-is-a-coffee-nation-as-it-is-the-most-important-beverage-in-Germany/.

In retrospect, it is easy to make sense of why REWE would pick Barilla as a loss leader. In practice, it is somewhat more complex to find the right loss leaders as it involves a lot of in-depth data mining. Back in the old days, pricing consultants had to manually go through the cashier receipts to look for clues about correlations between the items inside the shopping baskets and make educated guesses about what the lead items are that drive consumers into the store. What a tedious job! More frustratingly, it was practically impossible to find out the reasons. For example, we see that three products A, B, and C often appear together in a consumer's shopping basket. But it is still impossible to tell which one was the first to be placed in the basket and which products were added afterward to then fill the basket. In the era of e-commerce and ever-advancing big data technology, retailers are now technologically empowered to identify the order in which consumers put their products into the shopping basket in online shops. It is technically possible in brick-and-mortar shops too, if sensors are embedded in the shopping carts. Some leading retailers in China already collect and analyze shopping basket data in great detail to be thereby better informed about decisions to be made in offline operations such as the rationalization of product assortments, floor and shelf display optimization, and last but not least, pricing and promotion campaigns.

So far so good for the retailer, but not necessarily so good for the unwitting brand that is regularly put on promotion. I wonder to what extent leading suppliers such as Barilla voluntarily play along with the promotions. Over time, consumers are made to be aware of this and to buy only during promotion sales and eventually come to discount the brand equity. As is usually the case, the suppliers' bargaining power vs. that of large retailers is limited, not to mention that most countries prohibit suppliers from dictating retail prices for their products. It is no different online. Suppliers' pricing freedom is largely at the mercy of major e-commerce behemoths such as Amazon, Alibaba, and the like. That is why many brands run their own online shops in an effort not to have to rely only on the marketplaces, where the cost of attracting traffic is getting higher and higher. Social media or influencer marketing may open new opportunities for the suppliers. How to play it smart while fostering long-term customer relations remains challenging.

Lastly, let's turn our attention to the consumers. How can we protect ourselves from the tricks of the retailers? I have two pieces of advice. Firstly, keep track of what items appear regularly on promotion, and keep a large supply of these for the time after the promotion is up. Secondly, resist the temptation by buying only the stuff that is on the shopping list that you note down beforehand.

Remember This!

- Retailers frequently use established brands as loss-leaders to increase traffic into their stores and reply on sales of more profitable goods to make money.
- It may not be in the best interest of the brands that are frequently used as loss-leaders; the long-term impact on brand equity remains unclear.
- Consumers can prevent themselves from falling into the trap by making a shopping list and sticking to it.

A Pricing Perspective on Double Eleven

What You Will Discover?

Buy it! Buy it! Buy it!

Alibaba's Double Eleven shopping festival is huge, much bigger than its western counterpart, Black Friday. Since its inception in 2009, it has been playing a pivotal role in (re-)shaping the retail landscape in China. Among others, aggressive pricing has fueled the growth of Double Eleven. It is not uncommon to see consumers start filling up their shopping carts in the months ahead and to wait for the discounts on Double Eleven before checkout. Discounts, once a powerful growth tool, have been losing appeal to consumers. How should the successful story of Double Eleven continue to be written? How should merchants and brands react? Here is my pricing perspective.

The Black Friday shopping season has just closed doors. Black Friday is an informal name for the Friday following Thanksgiving Day in the United States, which is celebrated on the fourth Thursday of November. The day after Thanksgiving has been regarded as the beginning of America's Christmas shopping season ever since 1952, although the term "Black Friday" was not widely used until in more recent decades.[1] Nowadays Black Friday has also become popular in about twenty countries around the world, notably in the European and Middle East countries.

Black Friday was once a phenomenon in China, but it was never big. Inspired by Black Friday, the Chinese invented their own version of a shopping festival, the Singles' Day, which is celebrated on 11 November every year.

---

[1] https://en.wikipedia.org/wiki/Black_Friday_(shopping).

© Springer Nature Switzerland AG 2020
J. Y. Yang, *The Pricing Puzzle*, https://doi.org/10.1007/978-3-030-50777-0_11

The selection of the date 11.11 was meant to be a word play hinting at singles. Alibaba inaugurated the festival in 2009, to appeal to mainly single young people. But over the years, it became so successful that it turned into a nation-wide shopping fiesta in which all e-commerce platforms as well as traditional brick-and-mortar businesses participate. As the customer base penetrates all age groups from various different backgrounds, Singles' Day is now more commonly referred to as Double Eleven.

Today, Double Eleven has become the most popular shopping festival among Chinese consumers. Brands from different scales take the occasion seriously, not only as an avenue to push sales toward lasting until the year's end but also as an increasingly important marketing and communication opportunity. In 2019, gross merchandise value, also known as GMV, on the Double Eleven day amounted to ¥410 billion, or $59 billion, i.e., a 30% growth over the previous year.[2] To put the magnitude in perspective, Black Friday in 2019 made $7.2 billion in digital revenue in the United States and $20 billion worldwide.[3]

Historically, Double Eleven's growth has been notoriously driven by hefty discounts. Starting as early as 1 month ahead of 11 November, all kinds of promotions will be seen around. The discount rules are becoming more and more complex and difficult to analyze, with various combinations of discounts, pre-payment, special offers, and conditions that may apply within a single store or across the whole e-commerce marketplace. In order to create impressions of good deals, many merchants intentionally inflate recommended retail prices to create room for deeper discounts. This (mal)practice has been reported on repeatedly in media in recent years. Smart consumers learn the game of the discount rules, trying to make the best of it. This takes hard work for both merchants and consumers, especially to the detriment of the former. Double Eleven is supposed to be an occasion of indulgence, on which consumers impulsively go on a shopping spree without weighing the pros and cons. Generally speaking, consumer rationality in shopping is bad for business.

Over time, merchants have also been trying to optimize their promotion strategy for Double Eleven. But tactics that aim to trick consumers will not last for long and may backfire severely, such as inflating the price tags before the shopping season kicks off. A good pricing strategy for Double Eleven starts with a solid understanding of what it is that would stimulate demand.

---

[2] https://m.gelonghui.com/p/322234.

[3] https://www.forbes.com/sites/johnkoetsier/2019/11/30/record-black-friday-sales-14-growth-to-72b-in-digital-revenue/#437af26affc4.

If a price deduction does not generate incremental demand, the merchant will be better off not offering any discounts. There are several indicators, based on which we can have a chance to determine whether a price cut will pay off:

- Is the product a necessity?
- Is the product not easy to substitute by another?
- Does the product serve a special use?
- Is the unit selling price lower than the average in its product category?

Affirming the questions above suggests a lower sensitivity of demand to price changes, in other words, lower price elasticity, and therefore discounting or any other promotional activity will make little sense.

Double Eleven has turned many of my friends into hoarders and changed the pantry loading behavior of millions of consumers. They habitually wait for Double Eleven and purchase half a year's worth of consumable necessities such as paper towels, laundry detergent, toothpaste, rice, and oil, just to name a few. It is only a half a year's worth because there is another heavyweight shopping festival on 18 June taking place every year, initiated by the e-commerce giant JD.com, in which Alibaba also participates. 18 June is JD.com's home base, while 11 November is Alibaba's, conveniently half a year away and apart from each other.

The demand for consumable necessities of a household will be relatively stable, provided that there is no big change to the lifestyle or size of the household. Price decreases will not create incremental demand but will instead trigger hoarding. Whenever promotions take place, customers purchase a large quantity to cover not only imminent but also future needs, especially when future needs are foreseeable. Customers make advance payments and load their pantries full in exchange for discounts.

It makes sense for customers to do this, whenever they see decent discounts. For merchants, today's sales are increased at the expense of future sales. It is a value-destroying exercise from a net present value (NPV) point of view. In effect, the discount rate in the time period concerned in the NPV calculation is substituted by cash discounts granted to customers today. In most cases, the latter is significantly higher than the former, resulting in a lower NPV.

As can be seen in Fig. 1, expenditures on household necessities in China routinely peak in June and November in the last 36 months. Before and after 18 June and Double Eleven, the expenditures shrank remarkably, suggesting that consumers have been programmed to make bulk purchases on these two major shopping festivals. It is also worth noting that annualized expenditures over the last years have been remarkably stable. In other words, the

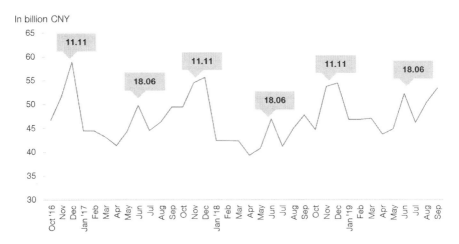

Fig. 1 Chinese national expenditure on household necessities October 2016–August 2019. (Source: National Bureau of Statistics of China)

promotions are directing sales to take place within a few days without increasing the total revenue for a given year, which has a severe negative impact on profitability. Some smart merchants have already become aware of the negative net effect and have acted accordingly. In the Double Eleven shopping festival in 2019, I noticed several product categories in which the leading brands refrained from offering any discounts, notably infant formula milk. Moms, as we all know, want their babies to be fed properly at all times.

However, what should worry merchants most is the change in customer behavior. Once the customers have developed a habit of purchasing only on discount, there is no easy coming back. The spoiled patrons will wait for discounts, and they will be dissatisfied if the discounts are not provided or not deep enough to satisfy their expectation. Therefore, caution is advised when giving discounts on household necessities, unless they are strategically used to build brand awareness, for example.

It is a different story with products that are nice to have but not a necessity, for example, vacuum cleaners, coffee machines, beauty devices, etc. In these product categories, discounts do have a real shot at converting hesitant prospects into customers. Dyson is an example in case. Its hairdryers and vacuum cleaners have been very popular in China, despite the fact that their high-quality products often cost several hundreds of euros and above. Dyson made inroads into China at a time when the Chinese middle class was becoming more self-conscious and more aware of their lifestyle. Against the backdrop of increasing appetite for affordable luxury, Dyson has been gaining steam in China. It ranked fourth in the category of small home appliances on Tmall on

Double Eleven in 2017 and rose to runner-up in 2018 and 2019,[4] only second to Midea, a leading Chinese home appliances manufacturer, which acquired German robot maker Kuka and Japanese conglomerate Toshiba's home appliances business. Notably, among the Top 10 in the category of home appliances, Dyson has one of the narrowest product assortments and is the only premium brand with a premium positioning. This is a great achievement and proves that specialization is a viable alternative to diversification. Its 25% profit margin[5] is comparatively the highest. Hermon Simon, who coined the term Hidden Champions, asserts that only focus leads to world-class quality. Dyson's success is powerful evidence to that.

Tmall is an important sales channel for Dyson. Let's take a closer look at the pricing of cordless vacuum cleaners in Dyson flagship store on Tmall. See Fig. 2.

All data was retrieved from Tmall.com on 3 November 2019, when the Double Eleven warm-up campaign was up and running. The first column shows the recommended retail prices of available models, followed by discounts and resulting discounted prices respectively, applicable only on the Double Eleven day. The last three columns relate to the units sold in a 30-day time period ending on 3 November, with the last two columns adding up to

	List price in CNY	Discount in CNY	Discounted price in CNY	Total sales in last 30 days	Sales at list price	Presales for Double 11	
V7 Fluffy	2690	700	1990	31,386	70	31,316	Available on pre-sales
V10 Motorhead	3590	600	2990	25,081	80	25,001	
V7 Mattress	1950	500	1450	5,143	392	4,751	
V11 Complete	5490	200	5290	4,062	228	3,834	
V8 Fluffy	3090	600	2490	3,269	3,269	N/A	Not-available on pre-sales
V10 Absolute	4490	500	3990	574	574	N/A	
V10 Fluffy	3990	500	3490	532	532	N/A	
V11 Fluffy	5790	500	5290	151	151	N/A	
V7 Trigger+	2050	500	1550	77	77	N/A	

Fig. 2 Price and sales of Dyson cordless vacuum cleaners in 30 days. (Source: Author's own figure; data retrieved from Tmall.com on 3 November 2019)

---

[4] 2018 Double Eleven small home appliance sales ranking on Tmall, https://m.jfq.com/news/1055.html; 2019 Double Eleven small home appliance ranking on Tmall, https://kknews.cc/zh-sg/home/ok9pbn5.html.

[5] https://www.zdnet.com/article/dyson-2018-profit-breaks-1b-to-move-global-hq-to-singapore/.

the total sales. The first four models can be pre-ordered at discount, while the rest are only discounted on the day of Double Eleven.

The actual situation is a little more complicated. Let's zoom in on two concrete examples, V7 Fluffy and V8 Fluffy. V7 Fluffy is an entry level model and a bestseller in the Dyson cordless vacuum cleaner lineup. It is subject to the biggest discount at 700 RMB among all. On Double Eleven consumers can buy it for 1990 RMB, i.e., 26% discount off the list price. V7 Fluffy is on pre-sales, but there is a string attached. The buyer has to put in 100 RMB down payment when making the pre-order. On 11 November, she or he just needs to pay the remaining 1890 RMB to complete the transaction. If one does not want to wait that long, then she or he has to pay the full price at 2660 RMB. As you can see from the last two columns in the table, pre-sales dominate total sales, suggesting that discounts are effective in triggering incoming orders. Offering the highest discounts on an entry level item considerably lowers the entry barrier, making the product more affordable for the mass. The choice of discount level is also conducive to new customer acquisition, as the actual retail price goes down to under 2000 RMB, which is a significant psychological price threshold.

As the product name suggests, V8 Fluffy is an upgraded version of V7 Fluffy. It features longer working time and stronger cleaning power among others. Its list price is set at 3090 RMB, i.e., 400 RMB higher than that of V7 Fluffy. On Double Eleven V8 Fluffy will be available for 2490 RMB, after a 600 RMB cash discount. I am not sure whether Dyson did price research before. Judging from my own experience, 2490 RMB is likely to be a psychologically important price point that looks much more appealing to potential customers while still not giving too high a discount away.

Unlike V7 Fluffy, V8 Fluffy is not available on pre-sales. Therefore, all sales recorded in the last 30 days were realized at full price. Compared to the pre-sale models in the first rows, the total from sales of the V8 Fluffy in the last 30 days is modest. If the pre-sales numbers are indicative of portfolio performance, V8 Fluffy will have a powerful thrust in sales on Double Eleven, when discounts become applicable. As a matter of fact, consumers are likely to rush to place the order for fear that the preferred model might quickly be sold out.

The example of Dyson vacuum cleaners provides evidence to my theory that a smart discounting strategy could fuel top-line growth. Yet the challenge remains: what if I do not have a portfolio as innovative and cool as Dyson's and the entire market seems to be price- or discount-driven. The very assumption that price dominates a purchase decision is bad and not well thought through.

To start with, customers do not get happier after the discount drops to below a certain threshold. Based on findings from my own pricing projects, the joy of getting a discount usually starts to wear off at around 30%. The law of diminishing returns (see definition in *Good Morning Coffee*) applies to discounts too! And even more importantly, the relevance of price for a purchase decision varies across product categories, also known as heterogeneous price sensitivity. Just imagine a shopping wish list for a second. On the one hand, there will be items like a limited-edition cosmetics product for women or a long awaited game console for men. These are typically high-involvement products, for which you have invested a significant amount of time, comparing different offers before you narrow these down to a dream product that you absolutely would like to own. You will be buying them anyway, be it at a 10 or a 50% discount. If there happens to be a suitable accessory available, you will probably grab it anyway, at full price!

On the other hand, there will be items that you only buy when there is a bargain offered, as there is no pressure on making the purchase. See Fig. 3 as an example.

More than 80% of Chinese consumers are out hunting for good deals in cosmetic and personal health on Double Eleven. Bargains are essential in order to trigger a purchase, although there is the threat that they become more of a required than a motivating factor. As a matter fact, in anticipation of discounts, consumers will watch the actual discounts more closely. The best discount is therefore a non-discount. As of Double Eleven 2018, I have seen more and more leading cosmetics brands offer special editions of products or bundles created for the occasion of the Double Eleven shopping festival.

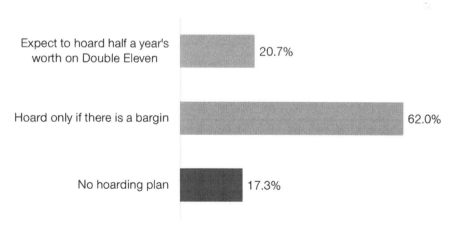

Fig. 3 Hoarding plan for cosmetics and personal health products—Tmall 2018. (Source: venndata, 2018 Tmall Cosmetics and Personal Health Report)

My central lessons for merchants as well as participating brands during Double Eleven: Don't get caught up in the trap of discounting too aggressively. It goes without saying that leaving out Double Eleven is not an option. If all of your competitors are participating, so must you. Therefore it is even more important to plan discounts and promotions shrewdly. We have seen too often that retailers are inclined to overreact and give away too much for nothing. Across-the-board price cuts are an absolute no-go! Communication of value should take center stage. The strategic war plan for Double Eleven and similar events has to be aligned with a holistic top-line strategy, one taking into account the full-year sales performance. It should incorporate factors such as product categories, roles, and other shopping events, and planning needs are to be based on historical data and customer research in order to fully understand the positive and negative side effects of discounts at each level.

As for consumers, my suggestion is to curb your shopping enthusiasm. Those nice-to-have things will be available one day with a better bargain, or you will let go of them eventually, if they are just nice to have after all.

Remember This!

- Shopping festivals like Double Eleven are maniacal events and have become discount jungles, while actual benefits for both seller and buyer are decreasing.
- Merchants should not blindly follow their competitors in offering discounts. A solid understanding of consumer behavior is essential if the aim is to develop an effective strategy.
- The best discount is a non-discount in that the merchant offers something that is unique and difficult to replicate.

The Premium Mass Product

What You Will Discover?

What is the correlation between Rimowa travel cases and Chinese passengers on a flight? What does it mean if consumers' appetite for high-quality products is increasing? Premium brands are confronted with the conundrum of right-sizing the client base. They are envious of the potential of the mass market while being afraid of losing their éclat if they do market down. Is there a way to reconcile premium goods and the mass market?

After an exhausting 12-h flight from Shanghai, the plane finally landed at Frankfurt am Main Airport. Rushing down the hallway and all the way through to the customs control – well, I walked at least 1.3× as fast as was my normal walking speed at the airport – I was the first (as usual) to arrive in the baggage claim hall. The prize for being this fast was a longer waiting time at the conveyer band.

Unfortunately, my suitcase came out late this time. While waiting, I amused myself with the observation that you can actually get a fairly good estimate of the percentage of Chinese passengers that were on board by counting how many Rimowa cases are on the conveyer belt. Admittedly, Rimowa is not in everyone's price league. But for people who can afford it, it is a top brand in the minds of many. Originally known as Kofferfabrik Paul Morszeck, Rimowa has always operated out of Cologne. Rimowa, a functional luxury item, is among the favorite local Cologne souvenirs alongside the iconic Cologne water.

A classic Rimowa signature aluminum alloy cabin suitcase retails for €840, while the majority of the suitcases offered by other brands are priced

© Springer Nature Switzerland AG 2020
J. Y. Yang, *The Pricing Puzzle*, https://doi.org/10.1007/978-3-030-50777-0_12

at below €200,[1] i.e., a price difference by a factor of greater than four. Nevertheless, the significant price difference does not seem to carry much weight with the purchase decision of the enthusiastic customers. Rimowa remains a top seller among affluent Chinese consumers.

Later on, I shared my observation on the anecdotal correlation between Rimowa cases and Chinese passengers on board on several occasions during my pricing seminars. It always elicits from the audience a good laugh, as many of them are indeed Rimowa owners. Admittedly, my sample size is small and hence subject to small number fallacy. But I think they still make a good example of middle to high-end Chinese consumers, for whom there are two kinds of suitcases on the market, Rimowa and the rest. Despite being much more expensive than the rest, Rimowa enjoys wide acclaim for premium and luxury luggage among the burgeoning Chinese middle class. Only until recently have there appeared aspiring newcomers like *Away* and others that challenge Rimowa both in quality and price. The premium luggage category is just getting more and more interesting.

Rimowa had been outgrowing the average luggage market for years before the French fashion powerhouse LVMH Group took over it in 2016. When you travel, you can see Rimowa cases everywhere at various airports around the world. Chinese consumers contributed a great deal to the strong growth of Rimowa. Rimowa is already huge in China; the growth of the country's middle class and an interest in travel is bringing in lots of new customers, according to Rimowa CEO's own account.[2] Germany is still Rimowa's largest market in terms of sales, but when it comes to its buyers, Chinese today top the list, followed by German and US nationals.

Chinese consumers are known to foster a *just good enough* mentality, which means that quality comes in second compared to functionality. But times have changed. China is transforming from a world factory to a world market, which opens new opportunities for premium products to become mainstream.

Let's take a look at a couple of additional prominent examples.

---

[1] Prices retrieved on 23rd January 2020, https://www.koffer-direkt.de/reisegepaeck/kabinengepaeck/auf-rollen/.

[2] https://www.scmp.com/lifestyle/fashion-beauty/article/3037859/rimowa-ceo-and-son-lvmh-head-luxury-luggage-brands-revamp.

Dyson

Dyson is just as popular and has become a household name in tier-1 cities in China. During 2018 Double Eleven shopping festival, named after the date of 11 November, Dyson's newly released hair styler named *Airwrap* turned out to be a huge success, despite its hefty price tag of ¥3690 ($548). It was reportedly sold out within 3 minutes on Alibaba's T-mall and after just 15 seconds on JD.com. In 2018's Double Eleven shopping event, Dyson was recorded as one of the 84 brands that cracked the ¥100 million ($14 million) record mark in sales within just an hour.[3] It was also named the best beauty appliance on T-mall the same year, enchanting millions of Chinese consumers. The British Dyson Group is a successful example of how manufacturers of high-quality household appliances can also benefit from the trend toward higher lifestyle-grade products among members of the Chinese middle class. Dyson entered the Chinese market in 2012. Three years later, the company's sales in the country increased to 244%. Dyson's cord-free vacuum cleaners were equally popular, with sales surging to 343% in 2016.[4] Dyson had 39.9% of China's offline vacuum cleaner market and 18.8% online. Either way, Dyson is China's biggest vacuum cleaner brand, an impressive feat for an imported premium brand.[5]

James Dyson, founder of the namesake company, was hailed as being "*Steve Jobs in the domestic appliances industry.*" He invented the vacuum cleaner, G-Force, in the 1980s. The Dual Cyclone technology used was considered the first breakthrough made since the beginning of the vacuum cleaner in 1908. Thanks to this invention, Dyson became a billionaire. According to a Dyson report, the company's EBITDA hit 1.1 billion pounds ($1.42 billion) in 2018, with a sales volume growing 28% to 4.4 billion GBP. An impressive 96% of Dyson's sales were made in regions outside of the UK. The company has witnessed a steep rise in sales since it first entered China in 2012. Its business expanded over three times in 2014 and 2015, respectively, and sales growth in China stood at 159% in 2017. James Dyson should be thankful to Chinese consumers for the title of the richest person in the UK.

Investing in technology has been key to Dyson's success, but so has pricing. While its products are expensive compared to similar ones from other brands, they're also affordable enough for many consumers in China. "Product

---

[3] https://www.abacusnews.com/tech/why-does-china-love-dyson-so-much/article/3037374.
[4] http://en.people.cn/n3/2019/0129/c90000-9542064.html.
[5] https://monitor.com.cn/2018%E5%B9%B4%E5%AE%B6%E7%94%B5%E4%BA%BA%E6%B0%94%E6%8E%92%E8%A1%8C%E5%90%B8%E5%B0%98%E5%99%A8-12082759558.pdf.

innovation (R&D investment) is at the root of Dyson's success, but Dyson has also done right in strategizing where to sell and how to communicate for the past couple of years in this country," said Rachel He, an analyst at market research firm Euromonitor. "It has now become an affordable luxury with easy access to purchase by adapting to market environment changes and learning to listen and talk to modern Chinese consumers".[6]

James Dyson was once challenged on the high price tags of Dyson products. His answer was classic: *How much are you willing to pay, if I solve your problem?* There is nothing left to be said.

Thermomix

I got to know about the brand about a dozen years ago. At that time, the management was anxious about the prospects of Thermomix, as the then newest flagship model was on the verge of breaking the €1000 price threshold. It was and is hell of a price for a kitchen appliance. I also wondered who would buy such an expensive kitchen appliance back then. After thorough analysis, the management decided to march across the €1000 mark. It was the right decision and a great achievement. Not all brands can surpass the four-digit price threshold as a growth impulse opening new doors to new customer segments. As far as I am concerned, I did not foresee that the Thermomix price would continue to rise while winning the hearts of housewives in Germany and beyond. At the time of writing, the newest Model 6 retails for €1395 in Germany.

The Vorwerk brothers Adolf and Carl founded a carpet factory naming it Vorwerk after the family in 1883, the predecessor of today's conglomerate still bearing that name. Vorwerk is known for its quality products as well as its direct sales business model. Thermomix is the star product of Vorwerk's portfolio, accounting for about 40% of the group's revenue. After years of expansion, Thermomix was confronted with a top-line challenge – its sale fell for the second consecutive year to 1.08 billion euros in 2018.[7] Growth in its home market, Germany, and the European Union by extension, slowed down considerably. In the middle of this challenging market environment, Vorwerk had to embark on a series of cost-saving measures, including lay-offs at its home base in Wuppertal. In the meantime, a production site in Shanghai was opened to meet the demands of a growing local appetite for healthy nutrition

---

[6] https://www.abacusnews.com/tech/why-does-china-love-dyson-so-much/article/3037374.
[7] https://www.huxiu.com/article/267125.html.

and international cuisine. China contributes to about 10% of Thermomix' global sales and is one of the fastest-growing markets.[8] With increased purchasing power, the Chinese of the middle class are longing for affordable luxury products in various aspects in their lives. They are putting greater emphasis on a comfortable lifestyle than the older generation once did and are willing to pay for a premium.

Vorwerk currently operates 26 cooking studios in Chinese cities, with 15 more to be added by the end of 2020. If Vorwerk succeeds in creating a success story similar to Dyson's in China, this should also secure jobs in Wuppertal. Even though there will soon no longer be a final assembly line in Wuppertal, important parts of the device will continue to come from the Bergisches Land: the motors and the blades for the Thermomix, both are essential to the superior quality of the kitchen aid and will continue to be produced centrally in the new plant in Wuppertal.[9]

We often contrast mass products with premium products. Mass products appeal to the majority of the market and have adequate quality but are imperfect in detail; premium products belong to the minorities, who can afford to demand perfection in every detail. Nevertheless, the abovementioned consumer goods examples prove that a premium product can also win the hearts of the masses and come to enjoy the lion's share of the market. Maybe a cutthroat price competition is not the only gateway to market leadership? Will premium mass products be the new norm for consumer goods? If I look at typical Hidden Champions, which are specialist in their niche fields, it is commonplace that they can enjoy both premium price positioning and the market share at the same time. In the B2B sector, the notion that quality should outweigh price has long been widely accepted.

If it worked for B2B, it should also work for B2C. I have always encouraged business owners to dare high-end positioning, all else being equal, my underlying assumption is that if the economy keeps growing (it always will if you think long-term), the accessible market of a high-end product will become increasingly larger, while more and more customers will trade a low-end product for an upgrade. In this sense, high-end positioning gives one first-mover advantage. And more importantly, we know empirically that it is much easier to go downhill (i.e., market down by lowering price) than to go uphill (i.e., market up by increasing price).

---

[8] https://www.sueddeutsche.de/wirtschaft/thermomix-vorwerk-china-1.4508147.

[9] https://www.wiwo.de/unternehmen/handel/rezept-fuer-neues-wachstum-wie-vorwerk-den-thermomix-boom-in-china-entfachen-will/24592950.html.

Last but not least, I do have a confession to make for full disclosure: my household uses products of all these brands above mentioned. Obviously, Doreen is a value shopper.

Remember This!

- There is likely a correlation between Rimowa cases on conveyor belt and Chinese passengers on board.
- The success of Hidden Champions proves that a premium product can also be a mass product.
- A premium price positioning is superior in the long run: if the economy keeps growing, the accessible market of a high end product will become increasingly larger, with more and more customers trading up. Brands that are associated with low quality will inevitably lose importance over time.

A Chilled Coke in Tehran

What You Will Discover?

In our daily life, we will observe that the same product can be sold at very different prices, depending on the occasions and locations. Sometimes we accept the price differences; sometimes we don't, especially when there is a sudden large price increase. When does price differentiation work? When does it not? What can we learn from the pricing of a chilled coke in Tehran?

Coke is one of those products for which the value perception depends only marginally on the intrinsic value of the product per se. Where and how the product is presented and sold determines the price level to a large extent.

I am quite used to paying different prices for a coke: €0.99 in a local supermarket in Cologne, €2 in a vending machine at the airport, €3 in a restaurant on the banks of the Rhine, and €8 in a fancy upscale bar in Shanghai, and the list goes on. You get the idea. Coke always stays the same (ok, admittedly the taste, no matter whether Coca Cola or Pepsi, differs slightly in different countries), but there is always something that gets added to the otherwise identical drink that justifies the price difference, for example, the glass, a piece of lemon, the atmosphere, and occasions, just to name a few.

None of the above examples fits an incident that took place in Tehran, the capital as well as the most populous city of Iran. The city impressed me in many ways.

In late spring 2016, I flew from Frankfurt to Tehran for the first time in order to deliver our first-ever project for a large state-owned enterprise. At that time, the United Nations had just lifted sanctions against the Persian Gulf nation after decades of boycott and isolation. Many infrastructure

© Springer Nature Switzerland AG 2020
J. Y. Yang, *The Pricing Puzzle*, https://doi.org/10.1007/978-3-030-50777-0_13

companies, such as telecommunications and oil companies, as well as many consulting firms from every part of the world, were (re-)entering Iran at that point in time. Among them, there were also many Chinese companies, such as Sinopec, CNPC (oil and gas companies, collectively known as two barrels of oil in China), Huawei, and ZTE (both telecommunication equipment manufacturers). Simon-Kucher & Partners was among the many Western consulting firms that entered the Iranian market then. Our team was tasked with developing pricing strategies and new price models for the latest innovations that the state-owned enterprise planned to bring to the market shortly.

My German colleagues and I plunged into this exotic country, having little idea what we would expect. Not surprisingly, we experienced a kind of culture shock from time to time. For example, we were re-directed multiple times to find the right entrance to an office building on day 1; the company's staff would just disappear at any time during(!) working hours for whatever reasons; the weekend is Thursday and Friday instead of Saturday and Sunday; fried foods dominated the culinary landscape (although McDonald's and KFC were nowhere to be found). It was very much of a kind of Newfoundland to us.

There was a neat and quiet Japanese park nearby our client's office. The park had been donated by the Japanese government and did have a serenity resembling that of Japan in a sparkling way. I detoured to the Japanese park after a quick lunch on a daily basis during the nearly 6-month assignment. Watching koi (brocaded carp in Japanese) in the Japanese park calmed my mind just wonderfully. More often than not, a coke would accompany me on my walks in the park.

After decades of being shut out from the outside world, the retail landscape in Tehran was left severely underdeveloped from a European or Chinese perspective. Convenience stores and supermarkets were non-existent back then. Mom-and-pop kiosks were the go-to place, if one needed drinks, snacks, or elementary groceries. There was this small kiosk just next to the client's premises, where I usually grabbed a refrigerated Pepsi before going to the Japanese park abovementioned. I would have preferred Coca-Cola, but this drink was hardly ever seen, which made Tehran basically Pepsi's territory. I don't recall exactly how much a can of Coke cost in Iranian rial (IRR). The country had been sanctioned for such a long time that the currency exchange rate fluctuated greatly even within the period in which I was stationed there, which was shortly after the ban was revoked. For the sake of simplicity, let's say that it cost about €1, which means it was not that cheap by local standards. Tehran City has a classic continental climate. April and May are already stiflingly hot, or even sometime scorching for European standards. As far as I was concerned, €1 was well spent for a chilled coke. The day after the start of Ramadan (early in July 2016, if I am not mistaken), the weather became extraordinarily hot, and the office was inadequately air-conditioned so that a cooled coke at noon was a very welcome drink and something to look forward to.

One day, as soon as the lunch break began, I decided to skip lunch and ran straight to the mom-and-pop kiosk I had been always frequenting. Only after going out with the Coke in my hand did I realize that something was different. It was the price! Counting the changes, I saw that the owner had charged me double the usual price! Trying to find out why, I turned back to have a word with the owner. It was a difficult conversation, as he was bad at English and I'm even worse at Persian. In the end, I came to understand that the price had been raised on account for the unusual heat, which consequently increased the pleasure derived from drinking the cold Coke.

That was an eye-opening moment for me, although I definitely hated it as a consumer. It was an interesting, textbook-like practice of dynamic pricing by temperature, which I had only read about so far.

As early as in the last century, Coca-Cola tested "pricing by temperature" in several markets around the world. The Coke vending machines were equipped with temperature sensors and embedded with pricing software to adjust price in accordance with the change in temperature. The ingenious price experiments did not find many friends, as consumers because of this protested against Coca-Cola, which the media pictured as the greedy merchant. The dynamic pricing scheme that I encountered in Tehran was essentially the same as that tried out by Coca-Cola, although on a more hand-operated level.

In spite of the miserable outcome of Coca-Cola's pricing by temperature experiments, its underlying logic merits a deeper look. By linking the Coke price to temperature, Coca-Cola was basically asserting that the price should reflect the value provided to the consumer. In this particular case, the assumption was that when the temperature gets higher, consumers find greater value in having a chilled Coke. In turn, the seller should be able to demand a higher price for the incremental value. Cost did not play a role here. Value for consumers should determine and drive the price. If you look around, there are plenty of examples where consumers are ready to pay different prices for the same product or service, without much hesitation:

- If one picks up a coffee at a convenience store or a bakery, it cost €1. For the same coffee, Starbucks would charge €3 and more. In the lounge of a premium hotel, it might cost €5 or €6.

- The entry tickets for Shanghai Disneyland cost 55% more on peak days than on normal days. The price differential goes up 80% during super high season such as Spring Festival and National Day. Nevertheless, the amusement park is still packed.
- Cab fares of Uber or Didi drivers could shoot up by 50% more than usual during peak times. Although people complain about the peak price, they will still be more than willing to be pay for it (especially when they are under time pressure to catch a plane or a train).
- Food menus can be (very much) more expensive in railway stations and at airports. As a rule of thumb, the closer you are to the point of departure, the more desperate you are, and the higher price you are willing to pay for a bottle of water or some mundane snacks.
- Airlines and travel agencies change prices dynamically over the year. You seldom hear passengers complaining about it.
- Hotel rooms in Tokyo cost over 20 times the normal rates during Olympic Games 2020 (unfortunately postponed to 2021 due to the COVID-19 pandemic).

The abovementioned examples demonstrate under what circumstances price differentiation is defendable, in other words legitimate. Specifically, my takeaways are as follows:

- Inelastic demand: if people set their minds on doing something (e.g., going to Disneyland with their family or going on a well-deserved vacation with old pals), price plays a lesser role in decision-making.
- Sparsity of alternatives: the concert has just finished; it is late at night. Public transportation is no longer in operation. In order to get home, you will have to take a taxi or walk. At the same time, others from the audience to the concert are also eager to make it home. Uber/Didi price spikes and you accept it.
- Proof of greater efforts: it is about fairness. Consumers are likely to pay more when they believe the service provider is going the extra mile (taxi trips late at night).
- Enhanced value perception: this is probably the most underrated factor. Value needs to be brought across to the recipient. In order to charge a higher price, the seller needs to make sure that the buyer understands the higher value of what is offered (a cup of coffee at Starbucks brings perks such as delightful atmosphere, free Wi-Fi, etc. that a bakery can hardly match). Otherwise it will simply not work.

In light of the analysis above, Coca-Cola failed for good reasons. Although consumers are likely to associate higher value with a chilled Coke on a hot day, they can choose to not pay it and just go shopping elsewhere. More importantly, it appears to consumers that Coca-Cola is taking advantage of them without putting in any additional efforts. This is the decisive reason that causes consumers to disapprove of pricing by temperature.

Even if the Coca-Cola Company were able to get away with the pricing by temperature scheme, it might not be in its best interest to do so. The optimal price depends on the shape of the demand curve. See Fig. 1.

For the sake of simplicity, let's assume that the demand curves for Coke are linear. The optimal price that maximizes profit lies at the midpoint between the variable cost per unit and the maximum price. Maximum price is defined as the price at which the quantity drops to zero. In scenario I, we observe a parallel shift of the demand curve to the right when the weather becomes hot, resulting in the increase of the maximal price. So it would make sense to increase the price. In scenario II, however, only the slope of the curve of the demand curve becomes steeper. It means that for the same price, there will be more consumers willing to buy a coke. However, the maximum price does not change. In this scenario, Coca-Cola will be better off keeping the selling price unchanged. So it is not so straightforward. One could also argue that there would be scenarios with nonlinear demand curves, in which companies should actually lower prices to maximize profit in hot weather.

Regardless of the shape of the demand curve, a sudden price increase will definitely not resonate with customers. I despise the kiosk which charged me

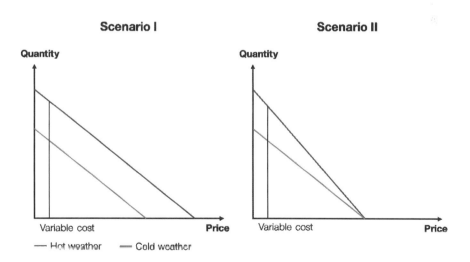

Fig. 1 Demand curves for coke. (Source: Author's own figure)

double the normal price on the grounds of hot weather. That said, I am not regretful about paying the extra price for the Coke in Tehran. After all, it provided me with a good story to talk about.

Remember This!

- Price differentiation is an important means when it comes to exploring consumers' willingness to pay.
- A solid understanding of what drives customers' perception of value and fairness underpins successful price differentiation.
- Even if customers accept pricing by temperature, a variation of price differentiation, it might not be in the best interest of the company to implement this, because the optimal price depends on the underlying demand curve.

We Love Dynamic Pricing

What You Will Discover?

Dynamic pricing is a topic dear to pricing professionals and much discussed among these. It is lauded as the state-of-the-art, supreme format of pricing. However, there is nothing new under the sun. Dynamic pricing used to be the norm 150 years ago until fixed pricing took center stage. When did dynamic pricing start making a comeback? What should we know about dynamic pricing nowadays? Is it indeed superior? Are there pitfalls that one should be mindful of?

Dynamic pricing is the new black in pricing. Everybody in pricing and revenue management jobs is talking about dynamic pricing. Role models such as Amazon have been known to make millions of price changes every day for a long time. Brick-and-mortar retailers are also embracing dynamic pricing through the adoption of electronic price labels which conveniently enable changes in the shelf prices during the day. Promotional prices can be rolled out temporarily and automatically reset after the promotion is over. Thanks to the advance of technology, price harmonization between online and offline channels has become possible.

Dynamic pricing sounds fancy and state-of-the-art, but it has been around for ages, as a matter of fact. Let's jump into a time machine and take a look at the history of dynamic pricing, also known as surge pricing under circumstances.

We are used to price labels, be they online or in brick-and-mortar stores. If you do not see the price label on the shirt that you like in a boutique shop, you will probably ask the shop assistant for it. Although price labels are commonplace these days, they actually did not come into existence till about 150 years ago. In the time when there were no price labels, dynamic pricing was the norm—every price had to be determined individually, as each customer had to haggle with the shop owner to strike a deal.

Fixed prices at that time were rare. The Quakers are believed to have pioneered applying fixed pricing in retail in the name of egalitarianism. The Quakers, also known as Friends, are a historically Christian group whose formal name is the Religious Society of Friends or Friends Church.[1] By charging the same price for every product on the shop floor, Quakers claimed to have invented a system that is fair for all, regardless of wealth or status.

Apart from Quakers, who used fixed pricing for the sake of fairness, there were also other retail business owners trying hard to get rid of dynamic pricing. Their foremost intention was to reduce the dependence on the highly skilled shop assistants. In the meanwhile, the introduction of price labels was supposed to improve the overall customer experience by reducing the uncertainty in negotiation with shop assistants. Once introduced, the fixed-price model became popular and was soon widely adopted. But then when did dynamic pricing crawl back into the business world?

Dynamic pricing first re-emerged in the airline industry in the United States about 40 years ago. The airline industry's seat prices used to be heavily regulated by the government, which relaxed the legislation during the 1980s. As a result, the airlines regained control over the seat prices.

In 1985, American Airlines pioneered the "Ultimate Super Saver" fare based on an algorithm called *DINAMO* (an abbreviation for *Dynamic Inventory Allocation and Maintenance Optimizer*), which was applied to 5000+ flights a day. Analysts initially thought it was the start of a price war. The company's stock price plunged. However, over the next 3 years, the company actually managed to grow revenue by $1.4 billion in total (Baltazar 2008).

Bob Crandall played a pivotal role in the implementation of *DINAMO*. He was VP Marketing at that time and was promoted to CEO later. He recognized a problem that had been plaguing the airline industry but that no one had really cared to take of it, namely, that many of the American Airlines flights lifted off with empty seats, while the marginal cost of filling these seats was negligible. In the meantime, there were distinct customer segments that showed booking patterns which strongly correlated with willingness to pay. For example, on the one hand, business travelers tend to make late bookings to retain flexibility of travel schedule while putting emphasis on arriving at their destination on time. They will go out on a limb for flexibility, which translates into higher willingness to pay. On the other hand, there are holiday-makers who pay everything out of their own pockets. Consequently, they

---

[1] https://en.wikipedia.org/wiki/Quakers#cite_note-2.

tend to book early to secure the bargains, willing to trade in less flexibility with flight times for lower expenses.

With these two typical customer groups in place, a self-reinforcing pricing mechanism was introduced—the earlier you book, the cheaper the airplane seats will be. It is not 100% accurate, as airlines learned to tweak the prices up and down along the booking curves (by customer group!). Over time, customers have been educated to not only accept the dynamic pricing rules but also play along. It is not uncommon for European holidaymakers to book their annual vacations a year in advance. As the saying goes, after the vacation is before the vacation. For business travelers, paying a premium is also widely accepted. As the name *DINAMO* (*Dynamic Inventory Allocation and Maintenance Optimizer*) suggests, the dynamic pricing algorithm aims to influence demand by means of price and non-price factors to find a revenue-optimal path toward having an inventory of zero at the end of the selling window. There are three general scenarios of inventory depletion in the airline industry. See Fig. 1. In layman's terms, the three scenarios depict how the airlines manage the limited number of seats on the airplanes to generate revenue.

Scenario I and Scenario II are sub-optimal. In Scenario I, the airline fails to sell all tickets by the time of departure, missing out on the revenue potential of the unsold seats; in Scenario II, the airline succeeds in selling all seats on the airplane with only one problem: it is selling out fast, hanging the desperate last-minute business travelers out to dry. The airline could also have made more money from its limited seats inventory.

Scenario III is optimal in the sense that the airline manages the booking curve to its full advantage. The seats are being sold at a pace that leads to sell-out at the end of the selling window. Dynamic pricing is the most important

Fig. 1 General scenarios of inventory depletion in the airline industry. (Source: Author's own figure)

lever one can employ to influence the shape of the curve. Selling the right seats at the right prices is crucial, whereas a profound understanding of customer behavior (of different customer segments) lays the foundation for implementing a successful dynamic pricing algorithm. Big data analysis enables identification of the booking patterns, but the revenue management professionals are still burdened by the task of having to design meaningful pricing rules and to then monitor the impact on a continuous basis. As cool as dynamic pricing may sound, it is still by and large driven by human intelligence.

It does not take an expert to tell us that the dynamic pricing algorithm of the airlines can still be improved even after decades of broad application. Have you ever come across such an announcement by the airline at the boarding gate?

We are looking for passengers who volunteer to change their flights to a later time. We will offer $xx (usually a decent three digit amount) for the volunteers. Please contact the staff at Gate 21 immediately, if you are interested.

What happens is that the airlines routinely sell more seats than are available on the airplane in anticipation of last-minute cancelations or people not showing up. I had one opportunity like this many years ago when I was flying from Frankfurt to Chicago together with my MBA classmates. While some of them took the offer joyfully, some of the more stubborn ones like myself preferred to stick to the original flight schedule. If you think about it, it actually constitutes a case of self-differentiation.

Despite all kinds of hiccups, there is no doubt that dynamic pricing has become the decisive factor for airlines' revenue and profitability. After the success of American Airlines, dynamic pricing soon became the standard pricing approach of the airline industry. Companies invested millions of dollars to develop algorithms that automated price changes according to changes in parameters such as seasonality, time to departure, destination, and many more.

In the years after this, numerous companies from other industries followed suit, railways in the late 1980s, hospitality and logistics in the 1990s, and telecommunication, media, financial services, retail, and even manufacturing at the start of the new millennium. More industries are expected to apply dynamic pricing in their revenue management in the future.

According to the experiences Simon-Kucher experts have made, leveraging dynamic pricing in the right way could bring about a 5–10% sustainable increase in revenue, which directly goes down to the bottom line. So there is a lot of money that can be made. However, caution is warranted for unintended consequences. If applied wrongly, it could also lead to disastrous

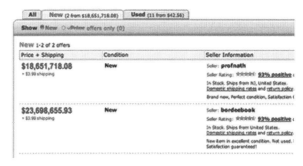

Fig. 2 The $23,698,655.93 worth fly book at Amazon.com. (Source: CNN, *Amazon seller lists book at $23,698,655.93—plus shipping*, 25 April 2011)

results. Dynamic pricing is not a kind of off-the-shelf solution that just needs to be plugged in to then let you solve all of your problems.

I mentioned Amazon as best practice at the beginning of this piece. Indeed, Amazon is regarded as the master of dynamic pricing. Well, Rome was not built in a day. Things can get tricky. Take a look at the following example from Amazon (see Fig. 2).

It is a fun story. In a nut shell, Amazon's point-of-sale dynamic pricing rule created a $24 million price tag for a book about flies in 2011. The hilarious result was rooted in Amazon's pricing algorithm back then—the machine checked the prices of two competing sellers of the book. An increase in the retail price by one seller would automatically trigger a price increase in the others. In the background, one equation kept setting the price of the first book at 1.27059 times the price of the second book; the other equation automatically set its price at 0.9983 times the price of the other book. Without an appropriate check-and-control system in place, the price of *The Making of a Fly* went through the roof, landing at $23,698,655.93 at its peak.[2] This example showcases the limitation of dynamic pricing. The outcome is only as good as the rules. Machine learning probes data for structure, either in a controlled or an uncontrolled way. The test for a machine learning model is a validation error on new data, not a theoretical test that proves a null hypothesis, for which a human mind is still superior.

We have come to realize that dynamic pricing is good for businesses, if applied intelligently. But how do consumers find dynamic pricing? Generally speaking, consumers tend to be more tolerant toward dynamic pricing practices that have been around for a while, e.g., airlines and hotels, primarily

---

[2] http://edition.cnn.com/2011/TECH/web/04/25/amazon.price.algorithm/index.html.

driven by capacity constraints and natural differences within different segments regarding their purchase behavior. In the meantime, we have seen negative publicity around more recently, AI-enabled algorithms as in Uber's surge pricing. Uber fares are calculated using an algorithm that is designed to lure drivers to areas where demand is high, whereas the users will be paying a higher than usual fee. The public got extremely angry when Uber's price surged 2.1 times during a terror attack in London in 2017.[3]

Dynamic pricing is not only limited to the B2C sector. It could also be an interesting approach for B2B companies which face fluctuating demand or volatile cost or both. I met senior managers of several companies in the B2B sector, who were talking about how their companies were going to embrace dynamic pricing. More often than not, I thought to myself that dynamic pricing was probably overdoing it for many companies. It reminds me of those manufacturing companies that like talking enthusiastically about Industry 4.0, although they probably have not even made it to Industry 2.0. A company that has not got the pricing basics right can hardly benefit from dynamic pricing.

In the summer of 2019, I got to know the CEO and founder of a chemicals distribution company, which at that time had a few hundred customers. The gentleman learned about dynamic pricing from a random article on the internet and has been fascinated by the idea since that time. He stopped me upon one occasion and asked me to recommend a dynamic pricing algorithm for him. I was bewildered. My immediate reaction was: Why the heck would you need one?

I tried to explain to him that he needed to do some homework as to customer profiling before jumping at charging differentiated prices, as a solid understanding of customer characteristics and past purchasing behavior precedes more intricate questions. I did my best but I was not sure in the end whether he was convinced. The fact is that even if he decided to go through with his dynamic pricing idea, he would have a very hard time in finding a machine learning solution able to satisfy to any larger extent his needs on the market. B2B pricing is characterized by complexities and human interference.

History always repeats itself. Dynamic pricing used to be the norm in retail before price labels were invented, as mentioned earlier. Since recently, dynamic pricing has been spreading from the airline industry to many others. The underlying reason for its use is, however, different. In the past, dynamic pricing used to be applied because of lack of information. Shop assistants and customers needed to negotiate before settling on a price. The outcome was

---

[3] https://money.cnn.com/2017/06/04/technology/uber-london-attack-surge-pricing/index.html.

dynamic and could be hardly foreseen beforehand. Nowadays the comeback of dynamic pricing can be attributed to an abundance of information. With the advance of technology, we are increasingly capable of profiling customers based on their shopping behavior and demographical characteristics, which enables precision targeting, individual marketing, and, in turn, individual pricing. Although dynamic pricing is to be a trend in the foreseeable future, entrusting it with a machine learning algorithm without knowing its limitations is risky.

Remember This!

- Dynamic pricing is an antique pricing technique with a history of over 150 years that was not revived until the 1980s.
- Solid commonsense is still required for successful implementation of dynamic pricing. Leaving dynamic pricing entirely to machine learning is not a good idea.
- Not every company needs dynamic pricing yet. Gaining a solid understanding of customer profiles is much more important than jumping at fancy pricing concepts!

Reference

Baltazar MB (2008) Revenue Marketing and its Application Within the Hospitality Industry: History and Future Development. In: Rothenberger S, Siems F (eds) Pricing Perspectives. Palgrave Macmillan, London

The Conundrum of Price Cut

What You Will Discover?

CEO: "Sales is declining! What do we do?"
  VP Sales: "Let's decrease price to recoup some sales!"
  Does it ring a bell? It is how companies act in reality. Whenever there is a sales crisis, managers feel pressured to decrease price, pretty much as a knee-jerk reaction. This can be a self-destructive form of behavior. When does price cut pay off, when doesn't? Are there better alternatives to price cut in the face of a sales crisis?

The case of empty parking houses is among my favorite examples in order to illustrate the relationship between price and demand in my pricing lectures for entrepreneurs and executives. It looks like follows:

Parking houses have limited capacity. Every single unused parking slot at any time represents a lost sales opportunity and profit foregone. We have this parking house operator which finds that the utilization rate of one of its properties in a central business district is extremely low on the weekends. So there is potentially a lot of money left on the table. Now what can you do to boost utilization and increase revenue? A knee jerk reaction would be to reduce prices to stimulate demand. Will it work?

When I put the question to the audience, the majority said *No*. Why is that? Presumably because I had before unduly framed them by showing them the impact of pricing on the bottom line with the help of the following mental exercise.

Suppose you find yourself in a deteriorating market situation, which of the following two options would you prefer?

1. *Cut price by 10% to keep sales volume from declining?*
2. *Keep price unchanged and accept 10% decline in sales volume?*

I don't know why a 10% decrease in sales should be more painful than a 10% decrease in price to many companies. They will prefer the second option, i.e., lowering price in favor of the sales volume, without really understanding the consequences. For the sake of simplicity, I set the scene as follows. In the starting situation, we have a product whose price = $10, sales volume = 1 million units, and revenue = $10 million. Assuming cost is equal to $8 million, we make a profit equal to $2 million. Further, we assume all cost is variable, which means cost is perfectly correlated with sales volume. See Fig. 1.

The impact of Option 1 is visualized below in Fig. 2a. In order to protect sales volume, we go down from $10 to $9 in price. What happens then?

Take a look at the green area, which represents the profit. A 10% price reduction would slash profit by half. Would you reconsider your decision? Wait, you have heard about price elasticity. Isn't it logical that we would have more volume coming in, if we decrease price? Fair enough. Let's see how much volume boost we need to make at least as much as profit as before? Check out Fig. 2b.

In a nutshell, it will be almost a mission impossible to be profit-neutral given even the seemingly harmless 10% price decrease. In order to bring in at least $2 million in profits with the reduced price, you would have to double the sales volume. It translates into a price elasticity of -10! Where should the massive increase in volume come from? Would you suddenly double the

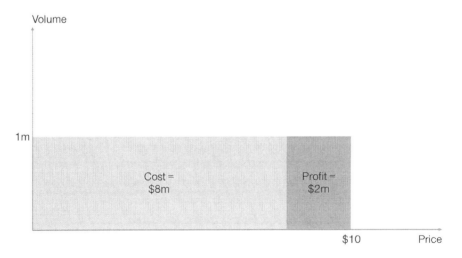

Fig. 1 Starting situation. (Source: Author's own figure)

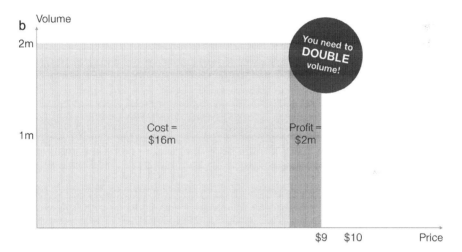

Fig. 2 (a) Option 1–10% price decrease without volume change. (b) Option 1–10% price decrease with profit-neutral volume change. (Source: Author's own figure)

customer base, because new customers would get so excited about the 10% price cut? Or would existing customers suddenly double their purchase orders? Neither of these scenarios seems realistic. We are also ignoring another possible negative impact, evident when we ask what would happen if competitors follow suit and decrease their prices, too. Unfortunately, a 10% price decrease would bleed you dry without bringing about any benefits.

Price decrease is often seen as the default action in a downturn. This was the case in the 2008/2009 financial crisis, and it is happening again right now in the middle of the COVID-19 pandemic 2019/2020. But past experience shows that it is more often than not the best decision to make. Do not get me wrong. I am not blind to the other forces that urge price decreases such as the need to support clients in trouble and maintain adequate market exposure, the pressure from work unions to keep workers employed, the fear of losing supply chain partners, etc. All in all, I am not against price decreases but encourage managers and business owners to be wary of the possible consequences to and ask themselves three questions before implementing the price cut. These questions are:

1. *Will I win new customers?*
2. *Will existing customers buy more?*
3. *Will competitors follow suit?*

If you don't have clear answers to the questions above, you'd better think them through and refrain from a price decrease till you figure out the answers. A piece of popular wisdom has it that doing nothing is also an option, and sometimes it is the better one. Maintaining price integrity in difficult times, i.e., not hurrying into price reductions, will prove to be a superior tactic in many cases.

So far we have seen what damages price decreases can do to the bottom line. It is only fair to take a moment to look at the flip side. What will happen if we increase the price by 10%? See Fig. 3a.

If we increase price by 10% while losing no sales volume, profit will climb up to $3 million vs. $2 million in the starting situation. How nice is that! Price is the most effective profit lever. Price increase usually pays off, unless you have zero bargaining power against your customers. By the way, if you have to pray the night before you raise prices by 10%, you are in a horrible business, according to Warren Buffet.

Then a valid and sensible question presents itself, which is: How much volume loss should we expect, if we increase the price? So let's do the math to see how resilient the profit potential from price increase is in case of volume loss. See the result in Fig. 3b.

Whenever we increase the price, volume reacts in a negative way (under normal circumstances)—less customers will be buying or existing customers will be buying less, or a combination of the two. All in all, we can afford to lose a third of the total volume if we thereby earn at least as much profit as before. We are looking at a price elasticity of -3.3, a moderate to high price elasticity. If managed well, price elasticity should be less in many industries. I am of the opinion that making a price increase is the safer choice if you are not sure whether to pick price decrease or price increase. The numbers are

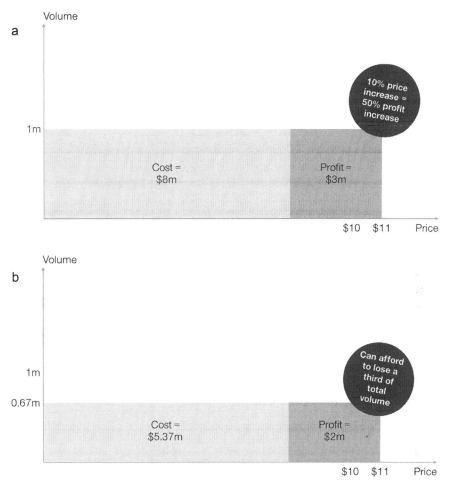

Fig. 3 (a) Option 2–10% price increase without volume change. (b) Option 2–10% price increase with profit-neutral volume decrease. (Source: Author's own figure)

more revealing than plain speculation. Do the math to be prepared or to be shocked!

Now, let's return to the empty parking house case, I believe that offering deep discounts on weekends is most likely not the right answer to improving occupancy. On the contrary, it could make things even worse for the parking house operator. Why is that? Because the drivers who have to park in the parking house on the weekends will definitely be pleased if they have to pay less than they were willing and expecting to pay; on the other hand, the central business district on the weekend is meant to be empty. Pricing is no magic wand. Price decrease will not create additional demand in this case. If I were the operator, I would probably consider increasing the prices on the weekends in the face of constant demand. For those that need to come over to the place on the weekend, the demand curve is extremely inelastic. In simplified words, it does not matter how much you charge, they will come and park on the weekend. It is a different story during the week, where you can use pricing to manage capacity in a more dynamic way. The technological foundation for dynamical pricing is generally in place these days. Nevertheless, common sense about the relation between price and demand is still much needed and valuable. Another possible solution would be a loyalty program which grants frequent parkers free parking hours on the weekend similar to and based on free night awards offered by many hotel chains to guests that come often.

There is a strikingly similar project example where price decrease fails to do what we want it to do. The client of mine, in this example, is a B2B retailer for miscellaneous factory supplies, keeping in stock a large number of items. The market landscape is highly competitive, as the customers usually have two to three competing suppliers in most product categories. At the same time, it is also a business with a very fat long-tail, meaning that the offerings of different suppliers have limited areas of overlap (there are overlaps, though sourcing through different channels could lead to significant price differentials at the end customer) and customers generally have little knowledge concerning prevailing market prices (because there is none in many cases, when it comes to industrial long-tail products).

It is not uncommon for salespeople to be closer to their clients than to their own organization, and they are tempted to give discounts to please their clients. In the meantime, the management also wishfully hopes to boost sales through price promotions. When conversing with the CEO of the B2B retailer for the first time, I told him about my gut feelings on the spot: price decreases are futile, as there will be probably no effect on volume at all. After having made this strong statement, I had to prove it. Among others, the project team looked into the instances of price changes in the last quarter. To my relief, the data proved me right. See Fig. 4.

In the last quarter, there were about the same number of price increases and decreases. As the business was growing fast, we were seeing growth in sales volume regardless of the direction price changes were taking. In the case of price increases, the retail price went up by 7.1% on average; when there were price decreases, the retail price went down by 3.0% on average. Interestingly, we saw a stronger sales increase, where the prices were increased. In the meantime, price decreases failed to boost growth, while destroying margins. In the price decrease cases, profit margins dropped by 5.5 percentage points. Price decrease is guaranteed to be a bad choice when demand is inelastic. For our

Changes in KPI	Price increase ▲	Price decrease ▼
No. of SKU	1,820	1,723
Average price	▍7.1%	-3.0%▎
Sales volume	████████ 68%	████ 23%
Profit margin (%pt)	▍6.4	-5.5 ▎

Fig. 4 Project case example of impact of price changes over last 12 months. (Source: Author's own figure; numbers are anonymized)

client in this case, the price elasticity in all product categories is generally low. We also noticed during the project that if clients are complaining about the price, there is oftentimes something else that they are not happy with, be it product- or service-related. Price cut is obviously not the remedy.

The CEO was so convinced of the results of our analysis that he soon hired a dedicated pricing manager as a conclusion of the pricing project. This is why we can proudly say that we are on the sunny side of consulting.

Remember This!

- Price has a huge impact on the bottom line.
- Do the math before enacting any price actions, especially when you are about to decrease price.
- Before decreasing price, you need to ask yourselves this:

  - Will I win new customers?
  - Will existing customers buy more?
  - Will competitors follow suit?

  Don't decrease price unless you have clear answers to the questions above.

Behind the Scenes of Price Elasticity

What You Will Discover?

In the last story, I touched upon price elasticity, which is arguably the most important concept in price management without delving into what it really is. As we are talking price, it makes sense to look deeper behind the scenes of price elasticity. It seems easy to understand but is often misinterpreted. So what does price elasticity actually tell us? How should we interpret price elasticity?

In layman's terms, price elasticity tells us by how many percentage points more products will be sold (either through more buying customers, or when more products are sold per customer), if the seller reduces the price by a percentage point, or vice versa. Formally, the price elasticity for infinitesimal changes is defined mathematically as:

$$\varepsilon = \frac{\partial q}{\partial p} \times \frac{p}{q},$$

where $\partial q / \partial p$ is the first derivative of the price-response function $q = q(p)$, where q is the volume and p is the price. By the way, I promise that this is the only mathematical formula that you are going to encounter in this book.

Price elasticity reveals the way that demand reacts to price changes. Suppose you know your price elasticity and cost correctly; you will then have found the optimum price to maximize your profit. In modern price management, one can hardly get around making a price decision without before that giving some thought to the underlying price elasticity. It is a must-have in the price

© Springer Nature Switzerland AG 2020

J. Y. Yang, *The Pricing Puzzle*, https://doi.org/10.1007/978-3-030-50777-0_16

management toolkit. But the interpretation and use of price elasticity are not as straightforward as it appears.

One day, a student ran to me enthusiastically during the break of a pricing class. In the last session, I talked about price elasticity and what it could do (in hindsight, I realized that I should have stressed what it could not do). It turned out he owned a furniture manufacturing company. Business was not bad, and the majority of the products were getting exported to overseas. But he scratched his head every time when he had to price a new product or adjusted the prices of existing products. The possible dimensions include design elements, wood type, the surface treatment, a great variety of accessories and design elements, etc.; this makes pricing decisions very hard work, which ended in guess work oftentimes in the past. He had been orienting the company toward his main competitors' price benchmarks, whenever possible; he would go up with these when he found out popular furniture pieces were being sold out very/too quickly. But should he follow his competitors' price moves? How would he be able to differentiate price changes across products? When would he reach the price optimum? These are just examples of the questions he wished to have an answer to. When he heard about the concept of price elasticity, he was so excited about it and thought that it might be the right tool for him in helping to make better price decisions. So we had the following dialogue:

He: *"What is the typical price elasticity in the furniture market?"*
I: *"I am afraid that a typical price elasticity does not exist. You will have to consider the following factors…"*

He was apparently disappointed. As a matter of fact, I am always reluctant to make general statements about price elasticities. Well, I could make up something. But it will not help much in reality. Even worse, it could be misleading. Like many other concepts in economics, price elasticity is a neat concept on paper, but its application in practice is troublesome and deserves caution. There are many (!) caveats to the use of price elasticity. In what follows, I will elaborate on three of the most common hurdles that discount or even destruct the power of price elasticity.

1. *You don't know what exactly the market is, to which the price elasticity applies.*

It may sound bizarre at first glance. How is it possible? Should it not be a no-brainer to know what market one is talking about? Hold your horses and let me spell it out. Price elasticity tells us the sensitivity of the demand change to the price change in a market, which needs to be defined. Depending on the definition of the market, you may end up with significantly different price elasticities.

Take the furniture market as an example. Are we talking about the entire furniture market? The low price market? The medium price market? The high price market? Or the medium to high price market? I bet that now you see why simply saying that the price elasticity in the furniture market is, e.g., -2 does not really get you anywhere. Even if you tell me it is the medium price market which applies, the boundaries or the defining price thresholds may be in limbo over time. The same is true for the price elasticity of the medium price market.

Price is just one dimension by which one can slice and dice the market. There are plenty of other dimensions such as geography, demography, and sales channels, just to name a few. Combinations of these different dimensions give rise to different market segments. Theoretically, you can still try to compute price elasticities for these market segments, as long as you have a cleanly defined market and supporting data. In practice, it is often a difficult task. Rather than pinpointing the exact price elasticities, I would be more comfortable with discussing the characteristics of segments, which would be indicative of the price sensitivity.

Well, if you insist that you have conquered the hurdle of the market definition, let's move on and take a look at the second hurdle.

2. *You don't know where you are on the price volume curve.*

The price volume curve tells you at what price point how much volume you can expect to sell. Does that sound familiar? If you have studied economics at college, you may recall a linear curve from your textbook. Wait, there are several types of curves which have different shapes. Check out the most common curves below. See Fig. 1.

No. 1 seems to be the most straightforward, where price and volume are perfectly linearly correlated. Because of the slope the price response function is a constant, the volume change in reaction to a certain price change is the same everywhere. Price elasticity increases as the price increases. The linear model is intuitive but can lead to erroneous conclusions in case of significant price changes, which would induce demand shocks.

On the price curve No. 2, the price elasticity is about the same level at every point of the curve. As one can see from the shape of the curve, the demand will stay rather stable past a certain price threshold toward a high price, while on the other hand the demand is extremely responsive to price changes in the

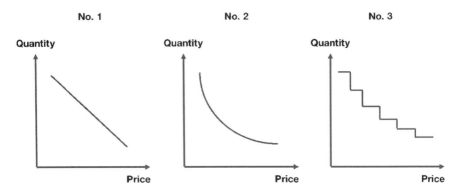

Fig. 1   Price response curves. (Source: Author's own figure)

low price segment. This makes sense because affluent people are much less price-sensitive in the high price segment. Due to the snob effect, we may even observe an inverse price elasticity, meaning the higher the price gets, the higher the demand. On the other hand, consumers in low the price segment are inclined to pay more attention to the price, because their purchasing power is limited, and they have to make trade-offs between purchases. To sum up, price volume curve No. 2 neatly reflects on the consumer behavior as a whole. But there is a small problem. The underlying assumption of the curve is that the price elasticity stays virtually unchanged across the entire price range. In reality, there are price thresholds across which the purchase preference and willingness to pay will change drastically. This leads us to price curve No. 3.

Similar to price curve No 2, the last price curve, No. 3, should come across as intuitive. It basically says that the relation between price and volume is not a linear continuum. Instead, it is better described by looking at it as made up of distinct segments. The demand stays flat within a certain price segment, where price changes would do little to the volume. However, once price falls at the either end of a segment on the curve, demand will change drastically. In this scenario, it is crucial for marketers to recognize the price segments and the corresponding price thresholds. A price promotion needs to hit a lower price segment to be effective, i.e., to trigger incremental sales volume. If it fails to do so, it will be just giving money away for nothing, because price elasticity will be zero.

The other side also holds true. A price increase involves little risk, as long as it stays within the same price segment on the price volume curve. The very idea underlies the popular 99 price ending tactic. Speaking from my own experience, if you are confident that charging $95 for a product will work, you should try and go for $99. Between $95 and $99, the price elasticity is likely zero, as we are moving within the same price segment. Customers may not even notice the price increase. But for the business owner, the 4% price increase (i.e., going from $95 to $99) can mean a 25% profit increase, assuming that the product has a profit margin of 20%. Just think about it.

If you have not yet lost faith in price elasticity, come and consider the ultimate hurdle.

3. *You don't know what your competitors are going to do about your price changes.*

Suppose you launched a price campaign of a 20% price cut. Knowing your product has a price elasticity of −3 at the current price point, you were expecting the price reduction to boost the sales volume by 60%. However, sales volume stayed almost unchanged. Revenue and profit dropped instead, an unfortunate result. You know for sure that the price elasticity is correct. So what went wrong?

The problem is you are not alone in the market. Unless you have a monopoly, how your competitors react to your price changes will have a fundamental impact on the outcome. In the abovementioned case, your main competitor became aware of your price action and followed suit with a 20% price cut on a competing product, which means that the price level of yours vs. your competitor's has effectively remained unchanged. In other words, your price has not changed, relatively speaking. Both you and your competitor end up with the same sales volume as before but less revenue and profit in the pocket, provided there is no incremental demand generated through the mutual price reduction, a phenomenon typically seen in durable goods in the B2B sector. A factory will not suddenly buy more tooling machines, just because the price has gone down by 20%. It will be a different story in the consumer goods market, where incremental demand might be generated as a result. But how incremental it is is subject to the observation period. Chances are that future consumption will be pulled forward because of the price cut.

Applying price elasticity is a good starting point when modeling the outcome of price changes. I have seen numerous companies making assumptions about zero volume impact of price changes (i.e., zero price elasticity) in their business plans and doubted the legitimacy of the over-simplification. As demonstrated above, assessing and factoring in competitive reactions in modeling the impact of price changes help arriving at the right conclusions. If you carefully avoid the pitfalls, you will find price elasticity a powerful price management tool after all.

Remember This!

- Price elasticity is an important yet often misinterpreted concept in price management
- There are hurdles to correctly interpreting price elasticity, because you don't know:
    - What exactly the market is, in which the price elasticity applies
    - Where you are on the price volume curve
    - What your competitors are going to do about your price changes
- Know exactly the context in which you are talking about price elasticity!

Profit Phobia

What You Will Discover?

When I was in college, I was taught that entrepreneurs take risks and are rewarded with residual value of their undertakings. But nowadays many startup founders think differently. The pursuit of profit has become secondary. It has become something that is all about growth, growth, and growth. Since when have entrepreneurs been ashamed of being profitable? What is the unspoken truth behind the curtain?

Tech unicorns like to talk DAU, MAU, and GMV[1] among other new metrics, which say nothing about the profitability of the business. Growth is all that matters for valuation, which is even equated with being the ultimate goal sometimes—namely, startup, scale, and cash out. This holds true especially for Chinese unicorns, a unicorn species that collectively shies away from speaking about profitability, as if it were sinful. I guess that the fear deep down is that once they turn profitable, they will be valued with conventional valuation metrics such as P/E ratio, and hence their fortune will become more predictable. For Chinese unicorns profit is taboo. Growth companies are great; profitable companies are mediocre. Scaling up to the critical mass within as short a period as possible is what duty calls for.

We cannot afford to miss out on the big opportunity. Profitability is the least of our concern, at least for the foreseeable future.

---

[1] DAU, daily active users; MAU = monthly active users; GMV, gross merchandise volume

© Springer Nature Switzerland AG 2020
J. Y. Yang, *The Pricing Puzzle*, https://doi.org/10.1007/978-3-030-50777-0_17

The founder and CEO of a Chinese tech unicorn once said that to me directly and insisted on this being the case. Scale is the mandate; growth is the mantra. No wonder that some creative and crazy pricing actions are taking place in China. The case of Luckin Coffee sneaks a peek at a phenomenon nowhere to be seen outside China.

The story of Luckin Coffee is spectacular and has become a role model for many up-and-coming Chinese startups. The coffee company was founded by a former executive of CAR Inc., a leading auto mobility provider in China, in October 2017, and went public on NASDAQ in May 2019. All that happened in a time window of less than 20 months, in which four stores were opened everyday on average. Rome was not built in a day; in our times, one might make the saying that a unicorn can go public within a period of 2 years.

Luckin's blue coffee cup is highly recognizable and iconic. In various promotional collaterals in the early days, well-known celebrities appeared in ads with the tagline: *Lovin' the cup*. Soon after its inception, Luckin Coffee went viral and raked in millions of customers in a matter of months.

In its prospectus for IPO, Luckin Coffee management discusses the business prospects as follows:

> *We are China's **second largest** (author's note: Starbucks Coffee is the largest) and fastest-growing coffee network, in terms of number of stores and cups of coffee sold, according to the Frost & Sullivan Report. We have pioneered **a technology-driven new retail model** to provide coffee and other products with high quality, high affordability and high convenience to our customers. We believe that our disruptive model has **fulfilled the large unmet demand for coffee and driven its mass market consumption** in China, while allowing us to achieve **significant scale and growth** since our inception…*
>
> *… China's coffee market is highly underpenetrated. Inconsistent qualities, high prices and inconvenience have hampered the growth of the freshly brewed coffee market in China. We believe that our model has successfully driven the mass market coffee consumption in China by addressing these pain points. We aim to **become the largest coffee network** in China, in terms of number of stores, by the end of 2019.*

As a matter of fact, it did it. By end of 2019, Luckin had 4910 outlets, overtaking Starbucks which had 4300 outlets as the biggest coffee network in China.[2]

There are several key messages worth looking at in this self-appraisal. Firstly, Luckin Coffee suggests that it is in a competitive race against Starbucks but is growing faster, though without mentioning its name explicitly. Secondly, it

---

[2] http://finance.eastmoney.com/a/202001021343452090.html.

stresses that it is a technology-driven company, not just another coffee shop chain. Thirdly, it invents a new retail model that allows for high quality and high customer convenience as well as high affordability. It all looks promising. But it is actually a tricky business. Let me walk you through the points in greater detail.

Competitive Landscape

Starbucks Coffee is by no means a direct competitor to Luckin Coffee. Starbucks successfully commercialized the third place concept coined by urban sociologist Ray in the early 1990s. The first place refers to a place where people spend time either working or relaxing, in addition to home (the first place) and workplace (the second place). As such, the sit-in experience in a store is quintessential to Starbucks' business model. In contrast, the majority of Luckin customers do not show up at the stores. Even more seldom do they drink coffee on the premises. The Luckin patrons are cyber shoppers ordering online and having their drinks delivered to them by courier. This is a stark distinction.

If you have been to the Luckin outlets, you can tell immediately that they are not really inviting on-site consumption. The seats in store are principally occupied by couriers and spontaneous walk-in customers, both waiting to take coffee to go. Luckin Coffee planned to open 2500 new stores in 2019, outgrowing Starbucks in the number of stores in China. But numbers are misleading: Luckin stores serve mainly as pick-up stations and as such have limited, simplistic seating possibilities, while the Starbucks stores are full-blown cafes of much larger size.

That said, Starbucks is wary of the ambitious contestant and is also getting ready to speed up growth, with the goal of having 6000 Chinese stores by 2023 and moving into the delivery business in a partnership with Chinese e-commerce behemoth Alibaba.

Although coffee consumption in China is still small in global terms, it has been growing fast over the last two decades. The overall Chinese coffee market size was estimated to reach $5.8 billion in 2018 according to a China coffee market research conducted by Euromonitor[3] and is set to continue growing in the years to come. Starbucks has been playing a pivotal role in educating and developing the Chinese coffee market. Until Luckin Coffee appeared at the horizon, the main contenders in Chinese coffee chains had been foreign

---

[3] Coffee in China report. Euromonitor. https://www.euromonitor.com/coffee-in-china/report.

brands. On the high end, there are Starbucks and Costa; on the low end, there are Japanese convenience stores such as Family Mart and 7-Eleven. The market price range for freshly brewed coffee starts at 9 RMB and peaks out at above 30 RMB. By pricing its main products between 24 and 27 RMB, Luckin Coffee seems to have found for itself a comfortable spot in the market, a price segment in which there are no notable competitors. See Fig. 1.

According to an insider who prefers to remain anonymous, Luckin Coffee internally considers the convenience stores more as being head-to-head competitors. It is true, if we look at the actual selling price. According to Luckin's own account,[4] in Q2 2019, the company sold 63 million cups of coffee and made a revenue of 66 m RMB, resulting in average selling price of 10.4 RMB. In effect, Luckin was offering almost 60% discount on average and undercutting even 7-Eleven and others on that level. Luckin Coffee is by no means a direct competitor to Starbucks, considering the very different price positioning it de facto has.

So why does Luckin Coffee look to Starbucks? The reason is that doing this has the halo effect of the undisputed market leader and it is then easier for investors to acknowledge and see this and to envision what scale Luckin will eventually reach. Exciting, isn't it? But Luckin envisions something even bigger, which leads to my second point.

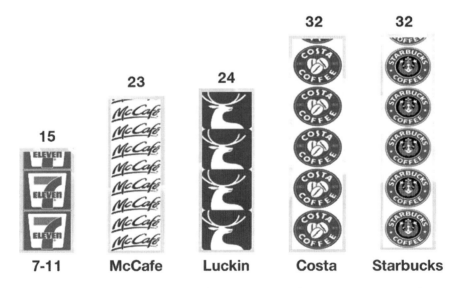

Fig. 1 List price of a large cup of caffe latte in RMB. (Source: Author's own figure, official app, store visit, October 2019)

---

[4] Luckin Coffee Inc. Announces Unaudited Second Quarter 2019 Financial Results.

The Technology-Driven Company

Profiling itself as a technology firm has a big financial advantage. It lures investors into applying valuation metrics that are conventional for tech companies (which focus on growth) instead of those for traditional food and beverages companies (which focus on profitability). Revenue and customer base growth dominate the valuation of tech companies. Profitability is only secondary, provided that the scale will translate into profits one day in the future.

One might wonder what kind of technology a coffee chain company is developing and applying. The prospectus is ready to hand and gives us a hint. Luckin Coffee refers to its technology as "the technology infrastructure including our mobile apps, systems and software. The development, upgrades and implementation of our technology infrastructure are complex processes."

Nowadays, isn't it expected of all serious fast-moving consumer goods companies to use some sort of technology infrastructure to acquire, retain, and foster their customers? Yet they do not call themselves technology firms. Although technology might enable them to increase efficiency or provide innovative value-adding service, it does not change the fact that the essence of the business has remained intact. Whatever technology a retail coffee chain adopts, its sole purpose is to serve coffee.

Luckin's engineered affiliation with technology has something in common with WeWork, which has gotten itself into deep trouble recently. WeWork claims to be a big data firm, calling itself the *Google Analytics for Space*. With the help of advanced analytics, it can optimize location selection, office space layout, functionality design, etc. In this sense, WeWork defines its business as SaaS, not *Software-as-a-Service* but *Space-as-a-Service*. All these fancy buzzwords add up to nothing and do not change the fact that WeWork spends $2 for every dollar it earns from its tenants and cannot make both ends meet (See note 4).

WeWork was once the most valuable American unicorn company with a valuation of $47 billion till 14 August 2019, when the firm submitted the IPO prospectus. With its financials exposed and in the spotlight, more and more analysts questioned the viability of WeWork's business model, and the valuation of the unicorn plummeted all the way down to $15 billion. In October 2019, the firm withdrew IPO. As a result, the disgruntled majority shareholder SoftBank ousted the founder and CEO Adam Neumann. At the center of the drama is that one came to realize that WeWork is no different than a traditional property operator which is invested heavily into fixed assets and has to deal with the mismatch between long-term lease commitment to landlords and short-term proceeds from tenants. Regus, the market leader in managed offices and space rental, is twice WeWork's revenue and yet profitable. In light of Regus' valuation of less than $4 billion at the time of writing, WeWork's valuation appears nothing less than exorbitant.

Similarly, Luckin is no different to other retail coffee chains. A reasonably healthy margin is needed to keep the business up and running. Although Luckin has been doing a good job keeping costs under control, it is facing strong headwind on the top line. Figure 2 breaks down the cost of a cup of Luckin coffee per Q2 2019.

The biggest cost blocks are those of the materials used, sales and marketing expenses (half of which are attributed to delivery expenses), and the operating cost. It is obvious that it is not a profitable business. Loosely speaking, the cost of materials and sales and marketing expenses are variable ones given Luckin's business model. It is not certain how much room there still is in order to squeeze the cost without compromising on quality. The average selling price of 10.4 RMB can barely cover the variable cost. Proven retail wisdom says that every outlet has to have a positive operating margin for a viable retailer chain business. There is no reason why Luckin should be an exception.

The New Retail Model

Luckin's retail model aims at achieving both high quality and high affordability; the latter is often a euphuism for low price in my eyes. I get alerted by *having the best of two worlds* kinds of statements. As is normal in life, you need to eventually pick a side. As much as I appreciate the overall experience of

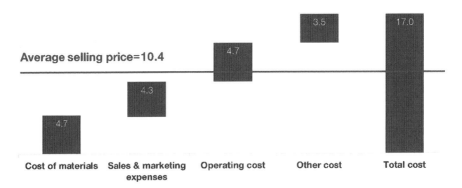

Fig. 2 Cost structure of a cup of Luckin coffee in RMB. (Source: Luckin Coffee Inc. Announces Unaudited Second Quarter 2019 Financial Results)

Luckin Coffee as a consumer, I am wary of its pricing strategy as a pricing consultant. Something is off.

The customers of a company that pledges high quality and low price will feel enticed to pay more attention to the price side of the equation, because that is the more tangible one. Due to a self-selection effect, their customers are usually really more price sensitive than the average customer. So, my observation is that the scale tends to tip in favor of price instead of value when conflicts arise.

Luckin Coffee's pricing practice is questionable, also because it leads its customers to expect ever increasing discounts like a windfall. Customers will come to take such discounts for granted and make increasing demands with the discounts.

In the early phase of a new business or new product launch, it is common practice to offer temporary discounts to attract/reward early customers. The discounts will gradually wind down, as the consumers learn to appreciate the product and the demand for it picks up over time. I consider this to be a legitimate pricing tactic. It is important for companies to have justifying evidence for their new products in terms of features and pricing. In this sense, early adopters pay to then serve as a recommending soundboard. In this light, I regard the early-stage discounts as a well-spent marketing investment (not as an expenditure!).

The coffee as such at Luckin Coffee is actually not bad, at least for my taste. The presentation and packaging also reminds one of a quality product, which in turn would justify its ranking in the same price league as Starbucks or Costa Coffee. With aggressive pricing, Luckin Coffee chooses to buy market shares that are not going to stick. The record-breaking growth trajectory of Luckin Coffee notoriously builds on lucrative and oftentimes unconditional discounts, which start with 32% at the inception of the business, soon go up to 50%, then to 72%, and finally to 82% at the moment of me writing this. As mentioned above, the average selling price represents a 60% discount on average, a price that guarantees loss on a per cup basis, without accounting for the fixed cost yet.[5]

I truly believe that there are not many potential coffee drinkers in a price segment of around 10 RMB or even below that which can also be converted into loyal customers. The first month retention rate of Luckin Coffee dropped to 17% in January 2019 down from 40% in the previous year. An iiMedia survey in March 2019 tells more or less the same story: at a price of 12 RMB,[6]

---

[5] https://www.huxiu.com/article/320489.html.
[6] iiMedia 2019 Research Report on Luckin Coffee.

37% of the respondents will not buy Luckin coffee; if the price goes above 12 RMB, Luckin will lose 50% of its customers. Deep discounts would attract customers that would otherwise not be customers. Once the discounts are removed or competitors offer even more aggressive prices, these customers will not hesitate to switch. The demand created through deep discounts is built on sand.

Once I was having a meeting with the founder and CEO of another Chinese unicorn in his office. Knowing I am a heavy coffee drinker and so he kindly asked his staff to bring us some coffee during the meeting. About half an hour later, I was surprised to have Costa Coffee handed to me.

I asked: "*I thought you would have ordered Luckin Coffee. Isn't there a Luckin Coffee shop downstairs in the lobby of the office building?*"

He replied: "*I feel it is inappropriate to treat my guests with Luckin Coffee.*" After a moment, he added: "*I would buy Luckin Coffee for myself, only if I had an 82% discount coupon at hand.*" The collateral damage of deep discounts goes without saying.

Luckin Coffee management is aware of the pricing challenge, as it states in the IPO prospectus that "*…our future profitability will be affected by our ability to properly manage the effective selling prices of our products.*" There is no easy way out, however.

The growth-at-any-cost mania is even more pronounced in the bicycle sharing market. In 2014, Wei Dai, a Graduate of Peking University, founded ofo together with four friends and alumni to provide bicycle sharing service for students. In May 2015, more than 2000 shared bikes appeared on the campus of Peking University. It was a bright beginning that did not end well.

As we fast forward to October 2019, we see more than 15 million users lined up on the ofo platform to have their deposit refunded. At the current payout rate, it will take approximately 120 years to complete the reimbursement. Countless bicycles ended up in graveyards in the aftermath of cutthroat competition between bicycle-sharing companies. At its peak, there were nearly 80 registered bicycle-sharing companies in China, all of which used extremely low prices to attract new users/switchers. As competition escalated, powerhouses such as ofo and Mobike literally paid users to use their service, a rarely seen negative price strategy.

Scalability is still very important for startups. But more and more investors are demanding a clear monetization strategy and a roadmap to profitability. SoftBank's founder and CEO Masayoshi Son admitted to having shown really bad judgment by investing in WeWork after the debacle in late 2019[7] and sent a clear message to entrepreneurs[8]:

Your dreams had better be profitable.

I hope that I will have better luck with Luckin Coffee than with ofo. I still have prepaid coffee coupons worth over 100 RMB sitting on my Luckin Coffee account, while I do not expect to live long enough to get my money back from ofo.

Remember This!

- No shame lies in applying aggressive pricing in the early phase of a business, which at times means paying a negative price in order to reach critical mass in a critical time window.
- But one should also have a clear plan on how to make money at the end of the day.
- *Your dreams had better be profitable.*
- Think twice before buying any prepaid coupons. In a single day on 3 April, Luckin Coffee shares plummeted by about 80% after announcement to investigate misconduct including fabricating transactions. Ironically, investors now can buy the shares with the same discount that the coffee company usually offers its customers. And unluckily, my prepaid coupons will likely go to waste again.

---

[7] https://www.theverge.com/2019/11/6/20951946/softbank-masayoshi-son-admits-wework-was-bad-judgement-q2-2019.

[8] https://www.aljazeera.com/ajimpact/softbanks-message-entrepreneurs-profits-matter-190927012445097.html.

iPricing

What You Will Discover?

There are two types of smartphones, the iPhone and all the others. iPhone is a category-defining innovation, and Apple is doing a good job at monetizing it. Nevertheless, the ever-increasing price of an iPhone has received a lot of criticism. Is Apple pricing iPhone out of the market? What was the logic behind of the pricing of iPhone 11? What does the future hold for iPhone pricing or iPricing?

On June 29, 2007, Steve Jobs took the stage at the MacWorld convention to announce that "We're going to reinvent the phone." He was right, although iPhone was not the first smartphone on the market.

IBM created the first smartphone in 1992, although the term *smartphone* did not get coined until three year later. *Simon Personal Communicator*, by which name the smartphone of IBM got to be called, was the first phone to merge the functions of a cell phone and those of a PDA (personal digital assistant). One could even run third-party apps on it. This powerful device had a price of $899 with a service contract included if purchased at launch.[1] You probably have never heard of it, because Simon was so far ahead of its time and had never came to widespread use.

In contrast, first-generation iPhones appear modest in technical specifications. These iPhones did not support 3G, had no third-party apps, no GPS, and no video recording, although these technologies were already available at that time. We all know what happened next. iPhone took the market by storm

---

[1] http://web.archive.org/web/19990221174856/byte.com/art/9412/sec11/art3.htm

© Springer Nature Switzerland AG 2020
J. Y. Yang, *The Pricing Puzzle*, https://doi.org/10.1007/978-3-030-50777-0_18

and turned out to be a category-defining innovation that literally reinvented the phone.

Since its inception, iPhone has amassed fans around the world, who ritually celebrate the release of new iPhones at the annual Apple Keynote with great enthusiasm year after year. In the last decade, iPhone has been setting the trends for the smartphone industry replacing the Mac as the icon of the Apple Company; it accounts for about 50% of total sales at the time of writing.[2] How well the annual iPhone release is received in the market has an immediate impact on Apple's stock price. iPhone sales have been growing with both rising shipments and an increase in average selling prices. The first iPhones in 2007 were available starting at $499. Ten years later, Apple priced the entry model of iPhone X at $999, representing a 7% compound annual growth rate. It is a remarkable accomplishment for a consumer electronics product, for the product category of which price deflation is more or less the norm.

Since Jobs presented the first iPhone more than a decade ago, smartphones have come a long way to having computing power comparable to that of PCs and have become indispensable for many people's lives around the world. Over time, a high-end market segment has come into being with people willing to pay top dollars for smartphones, while some of the mass market consumers distance themselves from iPhones because of the intimidating price tag. Speaking of myself, I have never been big on iPhone. Although iPhone is admittedly a very fine device superior to most Android devices in many aspects, I have difficulty in getting myself to pay that much money for something that is destined to become technologically obsolete in a year or two. I believe that I am not alone in thinking that way. A client in the smartphone industry euphemistically called me a smart shopper, as he noticed I was using a "budget" Android smartphone.

The premiumization of iPhones ran into obstacles in 2017. Although the new iPhone X did bring with it a bunch of innovative features, the price of a flagship model increased to over $1000 for the first time. $1000 is a significant psychological threshold which hardly any consumer goods are immune to. Intuitively, it takes much more convincing to buy a product the price of which grows, changing from three digits to four digits. It is a mental barrier to overcome, regardless of how great the product is.

In the next annual upgrade following the launch of iPhone X, Apple did not follow previous practice by then naming the 2018 models iPhone 11. Instead, the new models were named XR, XS and XS Max. I still cannot figure

[2] https://www.theverge.com/2019/7/30/20747526/apple-q3-2019-earnings-iphone-services-ipad-mac-sales-china

out what the R and S stand for and why XS is supposed to be superior to XR. The cheapest model is a 64GB XR, whose retail price was set at $749 (iPhone 8 was priced starting from $699 at launch), while all XS and XS Max models would retail near or well above $1000. One can tell that Apple fostered the ambition to push the average selling price up further, eventually gaining a foothold in the price segment above $1000. In the meantime, the lower end XR was supposed to cater to the more price sensitive customers while also fulfilling the shipment target.

iPhone fans were obviously not ready yet for the price increase. The demand had been lukewarm since the launch of the new models in 2018. Consequently, Apple became more aggressive with promotions to keep the sales volume up, while rumors of Apple cutting back on production were going around. In China, the biggest overseas market for iPhones, deep discounts were seen in various third-party sales channels to stimulate demand, bringing the transaction price of XS models back down to three digits, unthinkable in previous years when eager fans in China used to pay for new iPhones with significant markups, as they wanted to be among the first to hold the devices in their hands.

Sales pressure kept mounting on Apple, which had to cope with two fundamental challenges. Firstly, it was on the verge of pricing itself out of the market with its stretched pricing for its flagship models since 2017/2018; secondly, the price cuts on both its older models and new entry models no longer sufficed to drive significant additional shipments in the more price-sensitive segment. The situation was aggravating in that the Android smartphone manufacturers were catching up in both product innovation and user-friendliness, while charging a lower price, especially in the lower end segment.

Things did not change for the better for Apple as it entered 2019. In the first nine fiscal months of 2019, ending on June 29, iPhone net sales dropped by 15% compared to the same period last year.[3] In China, Apple's biggest overseas market, total sales declined by a whopping 20% over the previous period, while sales in other major markets stayed stable or continued to grow. Growth of smartphone shipments in China has been slowing down for nine consecutive quarters leading up to Q2 2019, during which time iPhone shipments dropped by 14% against Q2 2018 according to a report from the research firm Canalys.[4]

---

[3] https://www.apple.com/newsroom/pdfs/Q3%20FY19%20Consolidated%20Financial%20Statements.pdf

[4] https://tech.sina.com.cn/t/2019-07-30/doc-ihytcitm5732746.shtml

So finally on 10 September 2019 came the release of the long-awaited iPhone 11, which featured three lines named 11, 11 Pro, and 11 Pro Max, representing the entry, medium- and high-end models, respectively. Departing from the previous confusing lettering system, i.e., XR, XS, and XS Max, iPhone 11 returned to the conventional numbering system, to the delight of iPhone fans. Nevertheless, the improvements compared to the last models were modest, at a time when 5G network was getting made ready for commercialization, and rivals like Samsung and Huawei had already been showing off fancy foldable phones for some time. Apple's new iPhones appeared unspectacular, except for the fact that the triad rear cameras on the 11 Pro and the 11 Pro Max would probably take some time to get used to. On the inside, the A13 processor and 4GB RAM were the same on all models, although body sizes differed as with the last generation.

The pricing of iPhone 11 epitomized Apple's struggle with setting the course in order to move forward. The following charts compare iPhone prices at launch in 2019 vs. 2018 and offer a brief history of the pricing of iPhone entry models at their launches over the last few years. The first one concerns the US home market and the prices are denominated in USD (See Fig. 1).

The red flashes indicate where 2019 models are priced lower than 2018 models in the United States. iPhone 11, the entry level models, received a haircut of $50 across the board, making the entry models more palatable to the budget-constrained customers. In the meanwhile, 11 Pro and 11 Pro Max were kept at the exact same price levels as their predecessor models from the year before.

In the period from 2016 through until 2019, Apple introduced five generations of iPhones, with two generations, i.e., iPhone 8 and iPhone X lagging behind by a couple of months in 2017. The entry model price at launch in the

	XR	11	XS	11 Pro	XS Max	11 Pro Max
64GB	749	699	999	999	1,099	1,099
128GB	799	749				
256GB	899	849	1,149	1,149	1,249	1,249
512GB			1,349	1,349	1,449	1,449

Fig. 1 iPhone prices at launch in 2019 vs. 2018 (US, in USD). (Source: Author's own figure)

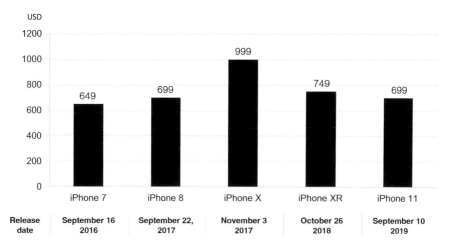

Fig. 2 iPhone entry model prices at launch in the United States. (Source: Apple, compiled by the author)

United States went up till November 2017 and has been declining since then (see Fig. 2). Pricing for the entry model went from $649 to $699 in the first 2 years, peaking at $999 with the full-screen iPhone X in November 2017, which was largely justified owing to a host of major improvements including an all OLED screen, Face ID and augmented reality capabilities, etc. Yet 2018 and 2019 saw the prices of entry models going south again. For the cheapest entry model, iPhone 11, which was introduced in 2019, the price stayed at the same price level as the iPhone 8 which appeared in 2017, although the former obviously offered better features. In the meantime, the most expensive iPhone model in 2019 (iPhone 11 Pro Max 512GB, costing $1,449) cost $500 more than the most expensive iPhone 8 (the iPhone 8 Plus 256GB, going for $949) at the time of its launch, resulting in a widening price spectrum of the iPhone lineup. The move alludes to the quest for a more profit-volume balanced approach by catering to both hardcore fans (high price takers) and value seekers (bargain hunters) with different products.

Apple adopted a similar pricing strategy in the Chinese market. Figure 3 (see below) is similar to the one shown above but lists the launch prices in China. Prices are all in Chinese Yuan. Similar to the US home market, Apple decreased the prices of all iPhone 11 models. Due to currency differences, the price reductions in RMB appeared even more attractive, as prices went down by as much as four digits. Unlike in the United States, Apple also cut the prices of the medium and high end models of 11 Pro and 11 Pro Max by 100 RMB, respectively, while keeping the lowest versions of 11 Pro and 11 Pro Max at the same level as the previous year.

Fig. 3 iPhone prices at launch in 2019 vs. 2018 (China, in RMB). (Source: Author's own figure)

Value seekers dominate the smartphone market in China. Only 10.1% of Android smart phone users paid more than 4000 RMB or 570 USD in the first 6 months of 2019.[5] A more attractive pricing for iPhone entry models could lure some undecided customers to market up, who would otherwise go for leading Chinese brands such as Huawei and OPPO/Vivo.

The initial feedback from the market was approval. According to CBN, a leading Chinese financial media group, the first day pre-sales of iPhone 11 on Tmall (Alibaba's eCommerce platform for authorized shops of brands) soared by 335 percent over the iPhone XR from last year, while pre-sales on JD.com (another eCommerce powerhouse known for consumer electronics in particular) was expected to skyrocket by a whopping 480 percent on a year-on-year basis.[6] Unlike the preceding generation, iPhone 11 had the same processor, i.e., an A13 bionic, as the iPhone 11 Pro and Pro Max but was much cheaper and thus offered great value for money. In a survey conducted by Sina (a leading Chinese news portal) on 15 September 2019, the biggest group of participants (37% of all) voted for iPhone 11 being a hit thanks to its attractive pricing.[7]

On a different note, I am skeptical regarding the impact of the decorative pricing on the more expensive models. A 100 RMB price cut on a product that costs over 10,000 RMB would achieve nearly nothing in terms of a sales increase. I can hardly imagine that an affluent consumer/avid iPhone fan would break into a sweat because of a 1% price difference. Most likely, the price reductions of iPhone 11 Pro and Pro Max will have little impact on

[5] https://t.cj.sina.com.cn/articles/view/6894743990/19af571b600100lgpo/

[6] https://baijiahao.baidu.com/s?id=1645065563613591425&wfr=spider&for=pc

[7] https://www.huxiu.com/article/318216.html

shipments, while losing out on millions of dollars in profit. The price adjustment of 256GB Pro might see some marginal traction in the market, as the price dipped under the psychological threshold of $10,000. Nevertheless, resellers might still sell for it for under $10,000 in retail to stimulate sales, despite Apple having kept it at the 2019 price level of $10,099. It would be a low-hanging fruit.

The appeal of the low-priced iPhone 11 might soon be contested, as the Chinese market leader Huawei followed suit in price actions. In Q2 2019, Huawei accounted for 37% of total smart shipments in China (27% growth over the same period in 2018), while iPhone ranks at No. 5 with less than 7% market share (down by 7% compared to last year) trailing Vivo, OPPO and Mi, according to an IDC report.[8] On 26 September 2019, Huawei launched its new flagship models Mate 30 and Mate 30 Pro. The lower version of Mate 30 was priced 500 RMB lower than Mate 20, last year's flagship model. During the keynote speech, Huawei's CEO went to great lengths to contrast the features of Mate 30 and iPhone 11. Merely looking at the specs, it was not hard to tell that even Mate 30 (starting from 3,999 RMB) was superior to iPhone Pro Max (starting from 9,599 RMB). Not to mention that the higher end Mate 30 models also supported 5G network, giving Huawei the first-mover advantage of being at the top of tech-savvy customers' minds. Specs are definitely not everything in a purchase decision concerning a high-end smartphone but they do have an impact on how potential consumers perceive the value of the product.

The aggressive pricing strategy employed by Huawei needs to be understood in a broader context. Earlier in 2019, Google revoked Huawei's license to use all of Android's services on future devices, thereby complying with an executive order by President Trump. Even so, Huawei would not be unable to offer Google services on its devices that were sold overseas. It cannot do so in China anyway due to Chinese regulations. The impact on overseas sales was predicted to be devastating: the users would not be able to access Gmail, YouTube, or even the Google Play Store on Huawei phones. According to Huawei's own estimate, 40% of its overseas shipments was put in jeopardy.[9] As a result, Huawei was to try hard to ship more within the domestic market to make up for the loss.

iPhone 11 is a great product in its own right. The uniform processor gives the entry model a strong sales advantage. According to Nikkei Asian Review, Apple requested its suppliers to prepare for a 10% increase against the original

[8] https://finance.sina.com.cn/roll/2019-08-06/doc-ihytcitm7307456.shtml
[9] http://news.mydrivers.com/1/637/637729.htm

production plan, being encouraged by the strong demand after the release of iPhone 11.[10] Logically, the additional production volume was mainly attributed to the cheapest iPhone 11 models.

But at the end of the day, this strategy may well back-fire, namely, if pricing continues to be the only remarkable innovation. After all, price is easy to emulate. From the broader perspective of Apple's business model, services have been gaining in importance. If the strategy is to lean in on services, a growing paying customer base is critical. With that in mind, the following years should see even deeper price cuts on lower-end models of iPhones. The jury is still out there.

P.S. The original piece was written at the end of 2019. In April 2020, Apple announced pre-sales of the new generation of iPhone SE as of 17 April 2020. iPhone SE 2020 was equipped with the latest A13 bionic chip inside and its price started from $399 in the United States and ¥3,299 in China.

Remember This!

- A great product starting from its inception, iPhone made leeway with its journey of premiumization in 2017.
- The price range of the iPhone lineup has been widening since then, as Apple is trying to cater to both hardcore fans (high-price takers) and value seekers (bargain hunters).
- Pricing is not all-powerful. The current pricing strategy only buys Apple time. There only has to just be "one more thing" for the success story to continue.

---

[10] https://asia.nikkei.com/Business/Technology/Apple-increases-production-of-iPhone-11-sources

The Milky Solution to a Luxury Problem

What You Will Discover?

Well-off Chinese consumers have been on a shopping spree worldwide. It has become even more convenient thanks to the rapid development of e-commerce. Foreign brands that are suddenly discovered by enthusiastic Chinese consumers find themselves confronted with a luxury problem – their production capacity is falling short of spiking demand. Infant formula is a case in point. How do milk formula brands cope with the luxury problem? Can pricing solve the problem?

Chinese consumers are constantly restrained by their anxiety. They always are, especially young moms, these are the most uneasy of all. They are concerned with the well-being of their kids and spare no efforts to provide the best there is to them. This starts with infant formula. Especially after several notorious baby food poisoning incidents, many young Chinese moms completely lost faith in domestic baby food products and became determined to find alternatives from overseas. From a European perspective, it may be hard to understand why the majority of Chinese moms shy away from breastfeeding and are so obsessed with formula. There is actually a good/bitter reason for that. I shall explain it later. But let's talk business first.

Wherever there is anxiety, there is a business opportunity. Due to lack of trust in made-in-China products and a concern about the health of their kids, Chinese moms set their eyes on milk formulas in foreign markets. Although this is a phenomenon in China that has been around for decades, at least, there is still this persistent perception that imported products are superior in quality and safer. Safety, in particular, is of vital importance to Chinese moms. Therefore, they will go to great lengths to shop for formulas in Europe, the

United States, and Australia, to name but a few, where they have confidence in the quality of what they are buying.

It is a luxury problem for a foreign brand, once Chinese consumers have set their minds on purchasing their products. It is a phenomenon called *demand shock*. Rumor has it that an otherwise unknown Australian farm in nowhere land accidently popped up on the radar of Chinese consumers' for having high-grade biological honey. The farm sold out its entire inventory in a matter of just a couple of days. This is the power of a huge buying group.

The Chinese consumer market is known to be colossal. Every single product market should theoretically have at least an annual turnover of CNY 100 billion. Consider the following back-of-the-envelope calculation: There are 1.4 billion people living in mainland China. It takes only CNY 70 per head per year, i.e., 20 cents on a daily basis, if you like, to create a CNY 100 billion market. Of course, I am not naive enough to suggest that the entire market can be compared to a reasonably accessible segment of the market. But the simplified exercise illustrating its size is meant to reflect the immense purchasing power of Chinese consumers, especially when they really want something a lot. Infant formula falls into such a must-have category for many anxious Chinese moms, who find formula all over the world except in their home country. The bias against Chinese formula is deeply rooted and at least partially justified given the horrifying past formula scandals.

The early-age baby feeding plan in China is totally different to the European standard. In Europe, moms and even dads enjoy extended maternity and paternity leave. This social norm espoused by governmental policy encourages new moms to stay at home and to bread-feed their kids for as long as possible (usually three years' leave for most non-working moms, as far as Germany is concerned). Consequently, infants in Germany are fortunate enough to get breast fed for at least up to around 12 months. In contrast to this three-year-long parenting period, Chinese moms have much shorter maternity leave, one that usually ends in the fourth month after a child's birth. I also notice that there is a different perception toward formula between Germany and China. German parents tend to consider formula as supplement to breastfeeding and as such as a Plan B; Chinese parents view formula as Plan A and feed their kids with formula far more extensively. It is not unusual for a five-year-old Chinese kid to be still partially being given milk powder, because parents believe it to be good for strengthening the immune system of their kids. Given the differences, the percentage of babies/kids being given formula in China is much higher than it is in Germany. Yet more importantly, the infant population of Germany and China are in two completely different leagues: in 2018 there were 0.8 million[1] newborns in Germany and 15 million[2] in China. If only 5% of the Chinese babies' parents were to decide to feed their children with German formula, the entire German market would be bought out.

Germany, known as the *virtue land* in Chinese, enjoys an unparalleled reputation for quality and safety among Chinese consumers. No wonder that many Chinese moms try to buy formula from Germany by all kinds of means, namely, via Tmall, online shops of the manufacturer, and various retailers, or through friends who live in Germany, or by asking complete strangers who work as freelance shopping agents. For a while, Doreen and I also used to run errands to shop milk formula in supermarkets in Germany and to ship it back to our Chinese friends. Just take a look at how the infant food export business to China has taken off in recent years. In a matter of 5 years, the export of infant food from Germany to China has grown by a factor of 10. The trend is likely to continue in the foreseeable future. Exciting for German infant food industry, isn't it? (Fig. 1)

Among all formula brands that one can find in German retailers, the most expensive brand, Aptamil, is the most popular one, thanks to Chinese moms' mentality of wanting the *best or nothing*. Aptamil is produced by Milupa Group, which in turn belongs to the French Danone Group.

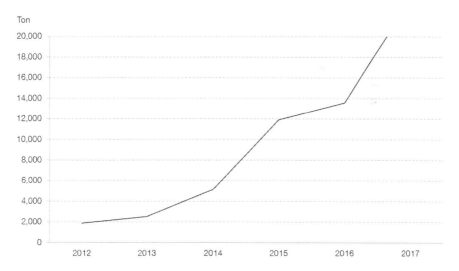

Fig. 1 Export of infant food in tonnage from Germany to China (2012–2017). (Source: EU commission)

[1] https://www.destatis.de/DE/Themen/Gesellschaft-Umwelt/Bevoelkerung/Geburten/Tabellen/lebendgeborene-differenz.html;jsessionid=8A6DA0756D50A456C54F6882FC3E572B.internet711
[2] http://www.chinatimes.net.cn/article/83639.html

There was once a period in which the shelves for milk formula in major drugstore chains such as DM, Rossmann, and others were frequently empty due to supply shortages, especially for Aptamil. During that time, it was not unusual to see signs on the shelves for formula: *limited to three cans per person/ purchase*. Unmistakably having specific customers in mind, the retailers printed out these notes in Chinese in addition to German. Above all, the retailers were forced to fend off shopping agents who try to procure not only milk formula but also infant food, cosmetics, etc. to then sell to consumers in China or via intermediary e-commerce platforms. In the case of milk powder, the shopping agents, who are usually students or housewives with Chinese background, make a few Euros for every package sent. As a father with infants at home, I also had my own frustrating moments staring at the empty shelves, knowing that the culprit was probably one of my compatriots.

Facing sky-rocketing demand from China, the Milupa Group was severely lagging behind in production. The spokesperson of the company described the situation as a demand storm from Asia that was sweeping across the company. In response to this, Milupa built a second factory plant in Fulda and has since tripled production. To say it in the company's own account, "We work non-stop—around the clock, 365 days a year. But it is still not enough".[3]

The Milupa Group also tried to market a new milk formula to Chinese consumers under the less prestigious brand Milupa. The *China* product line deliberately used a slightly different formula and Chinese labels in order to appeal to the Chinese moms. It has practically the same quality grade as Aptamil and was supposed to serve the Chinese babies better with its adapted formula. However, it never flew off the shelves, because Chinese moms believed the Milupa milk powder to be an inferior alternative to its Aptamil equivalent. In this regard, the milk formula market for endeavoring Chinese moms resembles the luxury goods market. Consumers equate the price to the value; price is the most powerful indicator of product quality. Consequently, the more expensive the goods, the more eager the consumers are to buy them.

In late 2014, Milupa launched the upgraded line Aptamil *Profutura* that came in a different and optically more high-end package than its *Pronutra* line for infant milk from 0 to 9 months. I have to admit that the first time I saw *Profutura* products on the shelf in DM, I was surprised by the shiny look and was speculating that it was primarily meant for Chinese consumers. After all, a hefty price increase came along with the package and the formula change to Profutura. It is €4 more expensive than the *Pronutra* line, which translates into a 25% premium. From a German perspective, it was quite a jump, while

---

[3] https://www.zeit.de/2018/32/babynahrung-diebstahl-kriminalitaet-international/seite-3

I would surmise that the price increase had little bearing on the Chinese moms' decision. On the contrary, many Chinese moms would go for the more high-end *Profutura* without hesitating. My speculation was validated by the changes of request for milk formula by my dear friends from my hometown. As a matter of fact, they often were amazed at how little they had to pay me for the milk formula I bought for them in Germany. The willingness to pay is obviously higher than the actual price the Chinese consumers are paying. While Germans take safe formula for granted, Chinese moms will go out on a limb to get it without saying a single word of complaint. The price premium is worth the peace of mind.

Milupa has played it well, very well in fact. Over the last 2 years, the supply of Aptamil has stabilized visibly. Aptamil has since seldom been out of stock on the shelves; the signs indicating a "*three cans only*" restriction are long gone. My friends keep asking me to buy the more prestigious *Profutura*. So it seems that we are having a win-win situation.

My take-away from this: When confronted by an unexpected spike in demand, it is wise not only to scale up just the production; that is a no-brainer solution. While price an increase remains a tempting thought, it is hard to implement, when there are at least two customer groups differing in willingness to pay. In the particular example of infant formula power, Chinese moms have much higher willingness to pay than Germany moms. As such, price differentiation alone cannot be the entire solution. Although a price increase on formula may not make much as difference to Chinese moms, German moms may feel hijacked and turn to an alternative choice of brand. Milupa was smart enough to couple spouse price differentiation with product differentiation, the most defendable format of customer differentiation.

P.S. I do have the weird impression that formula-fed Chinese infants appear to be bigger and fatter than my own breast-fed kids. Time will tell whether formula is good or not.

Remember This!

- Well-off Chinese consumers are eager to spend and are on constant lookout for trustable foreign brands.
- Consumers are willing to pay price premium in exchange of peace of mind, especially when the product in question affects their beloved.
- Price differentiation is most powerful when it is coupled with product differentiation.

The Coffee Revolution

What You Will Discover?

Nestle looks back on a history of over 150 years and has been the largest food company in the world, measured by revenue as well as other metrics, since 2014. It is a role model of reinventing itself and proof that elephants can dance. The jewel in the crown is Nespresso, which exemplifies what customer-centricity means and how it pays off. So what is their secret recipe for success? How does Nespresso optimize its offerings building around customer value?

I promise that this is the last piece about coffee in this book. But it is worth it.

Early one morning in Beijing, I went into the hotel lounge to grab a coffee to go before my departure. Hotel staff kindly offered to help. I rejected, as I preferred to do it by myself. After all, I was familiar with the coffee system well enough. It was a professional grade coffee machine by Nespresso.[1] This shiny silver machine would remind one of a classic barista machine made in Italy. In fact, it is not Italian but Swiss, and it actually uses industrialized coffee capsules instead of coffee beans as input.

As far as I can tell, Nespresso is all the rage. Recently, I have been seeing it everywhere, in offices, restaurants, hotel lounges, and friends' homes. The ingenious coffee machine system Nespresso developed has won over millions of fans all over the world. As chic and modern as the brand may appear, it boasts having a profound history that dates back to 1986, as a sub-brand of Nestle headquartered in Switzerland. Its mother company, Nestle Group, is one of the world's largest food manufacturers. Henri Nestle founded the

---

[1] https://en.wikipedia.org/wiki/Nespresso

© Springer Nature Switzerland AG 2020
J. Y. Yang, *The Pricing Puzzle*, https://doi.org/10.1007/978-3-030-50777-0_20

company, specializing in baby products, in Switzerland in 1867. On 1 April 1928, Nestle introduced the world's first instant coffee. Today, Nestle Coffee is ranked as the world's most valuable coffee brand, with nine sub-brands under its umbrella. It is estimated that in every second 4,500 cups of Nestle coffee are consumed.

In recent years, Nespresso has been one of the Nestle's fastest-growing as well as most profitable brands. Nestle does not disclose the financial performance for Nespresso separately. But it is not hard to tell that it is a lucrative business by looking at the price premium that Nespresso is able to demand. Compared to branded grounded coffee powder, such as Lavazza, Nespresso is at least five times more expensive as per February 2020. When a bunch of Nespresso patents expired in 2013/2014, third-party coffee manufacturers rushed to bring to the market coffee pods that were compatible with Nespresso coffee machines. Different brands of coffee capsules mushroomed in grocery stores, priced at two-thirds of Nespresso's price or even lower. However, they never posed a material threat to Nespresso.

At the beginning, I was excited about the cheaper alternatives, too, imagining that they would provide me with more flavor choices besides offering a lower price. I was also hoping that Nespresso would lower prices due to intensified competition. Soon I bought a pack of third-party coffee capsules to try it out. My first impression was one of disappointment. The shell of the capsule was made of pulp instead of aluminum. Fine, the low-cost alternative had to save cost somewhere. On a more positive note, not using aluminum could also be seen as being more environmentally friendly. So actually it might not be a bad thing after all. Then I found out that it took me quite an effort to put the capsule into my coffee machine. It was not that the capsule did not fit into the coffee compartment but that friction impeded the movements necessary for inserting it, which was a bit annoying. And then the coffee tasted differently, as expected. Somehow it tasted strange. I started to doubt whether it had been a good idea to not use the original Nespresso capsules. When I lifted the lid and tried to dispose of the used capsule, I decided that this was the last time I had bought third-party capsules. The capsule shell was soaked which made it difficult to remove the capsule from the coffee machine. It was not worth it, I said to myself. That marked my only purchase of the alternative capsules.

In a matter of months, all the third-party compatible capsules ebbed away from the shelves in the supermarkets. Compatibility is in the eye of the beholder. It seemed that the majority of Nespresso clients thought like me and voted with their feet. The bottom line is that it is not easy to break into Nespresso's hold on the coffee system, which has evolved continuously since its inception in 1986. The years to come after the expiration of the patents continued to see price increases of Nespresso coffee capsules. The customers had to live with it, as there was no viable alternative.

There are also companies that try to emulate the whole of the Nespresso concept by providing not only the coffee machines but also coffee pods as well as accessories out of one hand. Recently I have come across at least a handful of Chinese startups trying to do just that. I am always curious about what they would be able to do better than Nespresso other than offering their products at a lower price. Based on what I had experienced, being cheaper is not enough to win over Nespresso customers.

Sometime in the middle of 2019, I came across the eclectic founder of a coffee startup company that offers a knockoff version of Nespresso single-service machine along with plastic coffee pods, so in a way a total solution like Nespresso's. When I asked *him* "Why would a customer choose your coffee machine over Nespresso?", he responded immediately (I bet that he had rehearsed this many times): "The coffee pods that we make are bigger than those of Nespresso. Our target customers are those who crave a big serving, a need that the market leader Nespresso is not fulfilling. "

Hm, this was not entirely true. Nespresso had thought about that a long time ago. I chose to be polite and did not tell him that he was day-dreaming. In 2014, Nespresso introduced the *Vertuoline* system in the United States and Canada. Unlike the original Nespresso coffee system, *Vertuoline* makes a variety of coffees of different sizes including Espresso (40 ml), Double Espresso (80 ml), Gran Lungo (150 ml), Mug/Coffee (230 ml), and Alto/Alto XL (414 ml).[2] The versatile large-portion line was rolled out to European countries, followed by other countries, starting in 2018.

But it also made me think. Nespresso has come a long way and looks back at a history of nearly half a century. There have been a lot of trials and errors down the road. The idea of Nespresso was conceived and implemented by a Nestle employee in 1976, without having much success in its fledgling stage. Nespresso founded a joint venture with a coffee machine manufacturer to cater to the B2B market in the 1990s. The venture failed and nearly caused the company to go bankrupt. Around the year 2000, Nespresso revamped its business model which laid the basis for today's success with an annual growth rate of around 25%.[3] It took the Nestle subsidiary ten years to break even. But after that, Nespresso has been able to accelerate its topline growth profitably.

---

[2] https://www.asianentrepreneur.org/business-model-nespresso/
[3] https://www.investopedia.com/financial-edge/1010/top-6-reasons-new-businesses-fail.aspx

The complexity of Nespresso's ecosystem (a trio of machine, capsules and service) deserves having an entire book written about just this. Innovations at Nespresso go into both directions, downstream toward marketing and sales, and upstream toward sourcing and quality assurance. In what follows, I shall reflect on my observation of what key success factors have led to Nespresso's topline success.

In a nutshell, Nespresso redefined the portioned coffee market and has been leading the market ever since. Many of the competitors are copycats. Customer-centric marketing approach is what sets Nespresso apart. At the end of the day, the competition is ultimately about who can stay on top in the minds of consumers in the product category in question. When it comes to the coffee capsule, Nespresso has a stronghold over that top position. There are several pillars that underlie Nespresso's dominance.

Customer-Centric Thinking

Starting out as an e-commerce business, Nespresso has a natural affinity to digitalization. Alongside providing an exquisite in-store shopping experience, Nespresso attaches great importance to the digital customer's journey, thereby developing and fostering customer loyalty. The Nespresso member club, now branded as *Nespresso & You*, is considered instrumental in having brought about Nespresso's enduring success. A Nespresso member is entitled to various benefits, rewards, and coffee-inspired discoveries.

To ease the pains in choosing from the broad coffee variety, Nespresso provides new customers with structured yet user-friendly guidance on how to select the right coffee capsules.[4] The nice part is that a recommendation for coffee capsules can be made instantly after the prospect customer has answered a mini survey consisting of six questions such as what kind of pastry one likes, what moments one associates with coffee drinking, whether one prefers black coffee or coffee specialties, etc. I like the approach very much. Nespresso even customizes the content of its shop by country, catering to specific local interests.

I have seen too many companies swamping their websites with product lists and detailed technical descriptions for these. Why would a customer care about how many great products the manufacturer has? A truly customer-centric company will not ever do this. Instead, it asks what customers wants and what they want it for, just like Nespresso does. Effective marketing starts

---

[4] https://www.nespresso.com/de/en/order/capsules/original/ispirazione-italiana-coffee-bundle-3-sleeves

from a solid understanding of customer preferences, which is also conducive to forging the customers' feelings of attachment.

Thoughtful Price Management

Nespresso has been constantly enhancing its product lineup, which differentiates mainly along two dimensions, i.e., the size of a serving and the coffee bean used. A third dimension that Nespresso systematically explores involves limited editions, which are available only for a short period of time. It is a marketing practice widely used by Japanese consumer goods brands. Nespresso has been coming up with new limited editions year after year. Efforts in product enrichment go hand in hand with a targeted price differentiation. It would have been easy to charge the same price across the board. Nespresso chooses to go the other way. While offering a diversity of products, it has built a price hierarchy of at least four layers (see Fig. 1).

The basic espresso capsule represents the entry price level. The larger portion Lungo demands a 12% price markup. The Vanilio with vanilla aroma

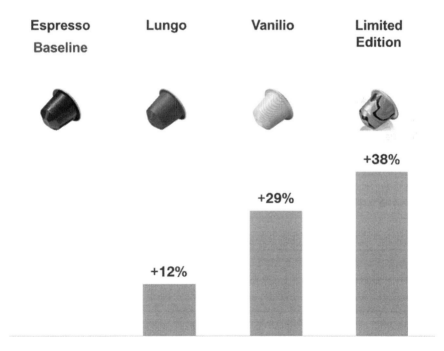

Fig. 1 Price markup versus baseline within the Nespresso Original Line. (Source: Author's own figure, data gathered from Nespresso China online shop on 6th February 2019)

costs 29% more than the basic product. The limited edition records the highest premium with 38%. Although the steps in price increase are big, if you look at the percentages in Fig. 1, Nespresso skillfully manages the price perception. On the one hand, there is vivid illustration on the webpage of each type of coffee, giving consumers the reason to believe that their choice is well grounded; on the other hand, Nespresso shows the price per capsule in the online shop. Even though the percentage difference is big enough to warrant a second thought, the price difference in absolute terms appears much more harmless. The most expensive limited edition *Nordic Black* costs 4.7 RMB. A basic espresso like Roma costs 3.4 RMB. A 1.3 RMB difference does not seem to be much a difference for your wallet, until you realize that the minimum selling unit is a sleeve which consists of 10 capsules. When you check out, you will find out that the minimum order size is 50 capsules, or 5 sleeves.

When something is considered too pricy and expected to scare away indecisive customers, retailers tend to communicate the price for a smaller unit. You probably have been there yourself too. For example, the fitness gym around the corner will communicate the price per month or even per week but will then charge the fees for a year upfront; the car dealer would tell the customer to buy a maintenance contract for her or his new car – "it is definitely a good deal to spend just a few dollars per day to have your new car covered."

Nespresso is also at good at bundling. It routinely rolls out themed trio packages comprising three sleeves. Check out this example.[5] In February 2020, Ispirazione Italiana Trio, featuring Italian style coffee, becomes available for €11.7 in Nespresso's online shop in Germany. This expresso/risotto bundle includes three sleeves, which are *Roma*, *Livanto Genova*, and *Venezia*, respectively. The unit price is the same for three coffee types, i.e., €0.39 apiece. It is not difficult to find that the price of the trio bundle is equal to exactly the sum of its individual capsule prices, which is not typical for bundling. As you already know, bundling usually comes at a discount. The construct is usually meant to be a bargain – customers are rewarded for purchasing a bigger shopping basket. As mentioned already, McDonald's uses bundles like the BigMac Menu to facilitate cross-selling, capturing customers' residual willingness to pay. In contrast, Nespresso does not have to offer discounts, because the bundles provide convenience in the sense that it makes the purchase easier. The nice, themed package can also be used as a gift. For the extra value that

---

[5] https://www.nespresso.com/pro/cn/en/pages/aguila420; https://www.coffee-time.at/fileadmin/templates/templated-ion/Angebote/Verkaufsliste_Nespresso_Operating.pdf; terms and conditions may differ by region

Nespresso offers, a discount is not necessary. Similar examples can also be found in high-end wine and nutrition subscriptions.

Remember the shiny silver coffee machine I mentioned at the beginning of the piece? It exemplifies how a company can serve both B2B and B2C segments and fence the two effectively. Arguably it is the best example that I know of. The brewing technology for both professional and household Nespresso coffee machines is essentially the same. However, the capsules are different so that the consumer solution and the professional solution are mutually exclusive. Cherry picking is impossible through smart product fencing.

Pricing for consumers and professional users takes different forms. Take Germany as an example, household capsule prices range from €0.39 to €0.47 apiece in the Original line. Professional capsule prices range from €0.34 to €0.38 apiece for professional use. The former is given out as having VAT included in the price, the price for the latter does not, so that the prices for business customer look lower. Even the minimum selling unit per coffee flavor is different. It is 10 for household use and 50 for professional. It makes sense that business customers will probably consume more capsules. So why not beef it up?

Yet the fundamental difference lies in that business customers will be entitled to the use of the machine for free if they commit to an agreed upon minimum consumption on a yearly basis for no more than five years. AGUILA AG420 is the Nespresso machine model I mentioned at the beginning of this chapter. With a commitment to using a minimum of 48,000 capsules per year, i.e., 4000 capsules per month, Nespresso will lease (not sell!) the machine to the customer and provide an all-round maintenance service to make sure the machine remains up and running throughout the leasing period. The number seems reasonable at least for the lounge of an upscale hotel, which easily serves over 200 cups of coffee a day, which makes 6,000 on a monthly basis. Customers have a two-fold benefit from this, namely, avoiding costs, i.e., having a better cash flow as well as having peace of mind as maintenance is taken care of by the vendor. What is the gain for Nespresso? The answer is that it leads to a long-term customer relationship, which provides it with more sales opportunities.

This strategy must have helped Nespresso gain presence in hotel lounges, restaurants, and offices around the world very quickly.

Nespresso keeps exploring new pricing models and techniques, while continuing to come up with great technical innovations. It combines the best of two worlds, when great innovation is combined with a sound monetization strategy.

Remember This!

- Innovations may come a long way. The sooner you capture the pain points of customers, the sooner you will become successful.
- Differentiation is silver; effective distinguishing well between different customer groups is golden.
- It does not matter how cool your products are; more important are the specific instances of use, which your customers associate your products with.

The Woes of MUJI

What You Will Discover?

A uniform pricing strategy across different regions is close to impossible in our era. MUJI learned a hard lesson in this regard. How should multinational companies go about doing their international pricing? What should companies beware of when changing their pricing policy?

MUJI used to be a hit. People liked to talk about how cool it is. Established as a globalized brand, the Japanese retailer designs, makes, and sells a wide variety of miscellaneous household articles, such as stationery, travel bags, apparel, dry foods, housewares, scents, and small appliances, just to name a few. Loyal customers around the world celebrated the minimalist and low-key design. By the end of August 2019, it was operating in 29 countries including in 359 of its own stores in Japan, the home market, and in 515 stores outside of Japan, of which 265 are in China.

Since the first MUJI store in China was opened in Shanghai in 2005, China has been a major growth engine for MUJI, accounting for nearly 50% of revenues generated overseas and close to 20% of total revenues at MUJI as of the 2nd quarter of the financial year 2019 (RYOHIN KEIKAKU CO., LTD 2019). However, recent years have seen growth in China slowing down, like-for-like sales dipping and profit deteriorating with each year.

However, probably the most worrisome news for the MUJI management is that consumers' enthusiasm about the uniqueness of the brand is ebbing away amid rising local competition, while its pricing practice is catching more public attention, in a bad way. A few years ago, MUJI China enacted high-profile price reductions across multiple product categories, which turned out only to

© Springer Nature Switzerland AG 2020
J. Y. Yang, *The Pricing Puzzle*, https://doi.org/10.1007/978-3-030-50777-0_21

be the start of a whole row of price cuts every year, even a couple of times in a year. The price reductions averaged around 20% and went up to 50% in some extreme cases.

Although the MUJI management claims to be doing the customers a favor by lowering the prices year over year, customers are turning their back on MUJI. Turnout in the MUJI shops has kept deteriorating.

As a regular customer, I have been witnessing MUJI struggle for years and cannot help thinking of IKEA. Doesn't IKEA have a strategy similar to MUJI if one take an outsider view? It seems to have much in common with MUJI – Both typically have simple and at times even demure designs, have strong influence in their home countries and widespread footprints across the globe, maintain a wide product assortment, and, last but not least, advertise in a noticeable way their noble mission, which is to bring quality goods to customers at an affordable price. Both companies have been being outspoken about the price reductions in their communication to customers. In sum, both companies follow a low-price strategy. But the outcome is strikingly different. How come IKEA is still popular and successful in China while MUJI is ailing? In spite of the low-price strategy, consumers do not first talk about the price when IKEA comes to their minds. So what went wrong with MUJI?

Let's take a step back to understand where MUJI came from. The brand MUJI or MUJIrushi Ryouhin in full means *no-brand quality goods* in Japanese. Just as the name suggests lie its humble beginnings as a subsidiary of Saison Group, a Japanese retail company. It championed the mantra of "lower price for a reason", creating goods of universal sleek designs like "water", at an affordable price.[1] The underlying strategy is built on three pillars, namely, those of selecting raw materials carefully, streamlining manufacturing processes, and simplifying packaging. All the cost reduction resulting from this is supposed to get passed on to the customers. It became soon very popular among Japanese consumers. The deliberate understatement of no-brand unambiguously accentuates the identity of MUJI.

In the following decade, MUJI fine-tuned its business concept and gradually expanded its footprint across the country, during which time, luckily, there was no serious competitor yet discernible. After successfully testing the acceptance of MUJI in London, MUJI embarked on a journey of internationalization in 1991. One year earlier, the ownership of MUJI was transferred from Seiyu, also a subsidiary of Saison Group, to the newly formed Ryohin Keikaku to concentrate on the further development of MUJI. In 1991, MUJI opened in the United Kingdom and also in Hong Kong. In 1995, it came to

---

[1] MUJI website, company introduction.

Singapore and three years later to France. Since the beginning of the twenty-first century, MUJI has accelerated expansion into foreign countries at a pace, until now, of one or two countries annually.

MUJI entered the China market in 2005. Chinese consumers swarmed into its stores and willingly paid extraordinary prices for the Japan-branded products, while the majority of MUJI's products were known to have been made in China. Until recently, Chinese consumers were reputed to be all in favor of cheap stuff and functionality while giving less attention to the frills. The success of MUJI in its early days proved that Chinese consumers also had a taste for lifestyle products and were ready to pay a premium for these. MUJI had a great ride in the years after having come in China. The business grew steadily and MUJI positioned itself as affordable luxury for cool people in China, a striking distinction in comparison to its standing in its home country. Until then, the story of MUJI in China was not much different than that of IKEA. In the early days, IKEA had also been regarded as an expensive imported foreign furniture brand, something not everyone could afford.

But then things started to turn bad for MUJI. With an increase in disposable income, more and more Chinese traveled abroad for work as well as for leisure. Nowadays if you had to guess where the Asian tourist groups which you run into in Barcelona, Munich, Paris, Prague, or Rome or anywhere else in the world come from, I suggest that you bet on China. Among all the places in the world where they like to go, Japan is a very popular travel destination for the Chinese. When Chinese tourists go into a MUJI store, they will find bargains there that are unavailable in China. One and the same item may cost twice as much in China as in a MUJI store in Japan.

Not only did Chinese consumers notice the remarkable price difference, smart merchants also did. It was not that difficult to find out which factories in China MUJI commissions to make its products. There were also copy cats of MUJI but they posed no serious threat to the Japanese retailer.

In 2013, Miniso was founded. It is a store chain that specializes in household and consumer goods including cosmetics, stationery, toys, and kitchenware. The founders used to claim that it was a Japanese company, as you might as well guess from the name. Even many Japanese thinks it is a Japanese brand. But as a matter of fact, it is a Chinese company based outside of Guangzhou.[2] MUJI is its role model. The layout and the feel of a Miniso store reminds one of MUJI. The late-comer also follows a low-cost strategy, but it is growing much faster than its Japanese benchmark. At the time of writing,

---

[2] https://www.cbnweek.com/articles/normal/22484.

Miniso has over 2,000 outlets worldwide, 1,200 of them in China,[3] outnumbering MUJI by a wide margin. Miniso posts a serious threat to MUJI as a viable alternative at a much more reasonable price. The competition has just gotten fiercer. Soon the big internet technology companies Xiaomi and NetEase also made a foray into MUJI's space, offering household items with a sleek design, reasonable quality, and an attractive pricing. Many of MUJI's suppliers are also supplying these late-comers.

In the meantime, low-cost fashion brands such as Zara and H&M, to name two of them, have taught Chinese consumers that foreign brands do not have to be expensive. They can be just as affordable as or even cheaper than local brands thanks to the scale of economy and an efficient global supply chain. This put MUJI in a precarious situation, namely, that of an identity crisis. In the eyes of a Chinese consumer, foreign brands are no longer eligible to be regarded as premium merely because of their country of origin. local brands are usually also better at cutting cost, offering products like those offered by MUJI's but at a much cheaper price for comparable quality. Especially, Xiaomi, which also looked up to MUJI as a role model, is known for its *maximum 5% margin policy* for any material goods it offers.

Confronted by the fierce competition, MUJI reacted. It announced a *new pricing policy* for China in 2014, supposedly "a change made for China." In the same year, MUJI reduced prices on 107 items by about 18% on average. The price reduction series was just beginning. By the middle of 2019, there had been 11 rounds of price reductions in the Chinese market.[4] We are talking about good two-digit price cuts here. Unfortunately, the price concessions did not help much. On the contrary, they made things even worse for MUJI. With repeated significant discounting campaigns, it there was more reason for consumers to doubt whether MUJI had done its best to offer the best price. The constant reductions inevitably led consumers to be first and foremost price-aware while becoming less sensitive to the efforts MUJI made in other areas such as those of portfolio rationalization, store layout optimization, product improvement, etc. What MUJI did with its new pricing policy is toxic in that it dilutes brand equity and blurs brand identity. The consumer sentiment has changed. MUJI is no longer as cool as it once was (cool brands do not offer discounts on introduction). The company started out as an *affordable luxury brand* in China (though not in Japan). Price was definitely not the reason why it was beloved. A price reduction of this magnitude essentially means abandoning its loyal customers. But for what?

---

[3] https://zh.wikipedia.org/wiki/%E5%90%8D%E5%89%B5%E5%84%AA%E5%93%81.
[4] https://36kr.com/p/5152834.

The Chinese consumer market is well-known for being fluid and dynamic. The low-price segment in any market is usually crowded by merciless Chinese players. This is no different in MUJI's market, considering that the entry barriers for household items are low. The sleek universal design that made MUJI fly off the shelves was what also turned it into a disadvantage, as Chinese latecomers learned and leveraged the design language quickly with an agile supply chain. Many of them claimed to commission the same factories as MUJI to produce their goods. There is no coming back for MUJI. Despite years of trying, it is just impossible for MUJI to go down to the price level of local competitors. After all, Chinese companies are second to none, when it comes to the cost cutting of commodity-type products.

In retrospect, it was not smart of MUJI to allow outrageous price differences between countries, especially considering China and Japan are neighboring countries reachable within two hours by flight. Leading multinational companies have long recognized the importance of keeping international price corridor under control. Louis Vuitton and Gucci, for example, actively cut retail prices in China following Chinese government's decision to lower import duties in 2018.[5] High prices in a foreign market may seem lucrative when viewed in isolation. But as long as the goods are movable, too large a price differential causes disgruntlement among consumers and leads to there being grey imports.

Starting off from a similar situation, IKEA has coped much better than MUJI in China, IKEA also has been reducing prices over the years. But it proactively communicates to the public that this is due to the fact that IKEA is trying hard to pass on the gains from cost optimization to the end consumers. In contrast, MUJI's price reductions have been unwillingly forced on them by competitors. The motivation making for price concession makes a big difference. Guess which brand of the two a consumer would prefer?

I empathize with MUJI. As a pioneer in its category, it had alternative options other than outright price concessions. Price concession alone was the wrong answer to changes in consumer sentiment. By implementing price reductions over consecutive years, MUJI has effectively confirmed the legitimacy of the latecomer competitors in its space. The irony is that the latecomers succeed in making goods at a more affordable price, the exact mantra that made MUJI successful.

---

[5] https://jingdaily.com/gucci-cut-prices/.

Remember This!

- Multinational companies need a coherent pricing strategy across regions.
- If you can solve a problem with price, it is not a big problem.
- Be careful with price decreases. There is no easy coming back.

Reference

RYOHIN KEIKAKU CO., LTD. First Half FY2019 (Mar–Aug 2019) Business Results Briefing.

Why Do We Want Price Increases?

What You Will Discover?

No consumer of sound mind would say that she or he loves price increases. Who wants to pay more for less? Governments or central banks around the world keep a close eye on keeping inflation at bay. Nevertheless, there are good reasons why we as consumers would actually want to have price increases. You will figure it out why it is the case in this story.

Since my childhood, grocery prices have been a recurring and beloved topic on dining tables with families. I grew up during a period in which the supply of non-staple foods was unstable, which in turn led to frequent price hikes. Mr. Zhu Rongji, the mayor of Shanghai, who was promoted to premier, was credited for initiating the *grocery shopping project* which succeeded in smoothing supplies and containing price shocks in the 1980s. No wonder that people keep talking about the prices on farmers' markets. In essence, it is not much different than the Brits' small talks about weather. People like to talk about things that are always there and have a direct impact on their lives.

Since then there has been significant improvement in both the quantity and the variety of food choices. The development of the Engel coefficient in China cannot be more telling. The Engel coefficient measures food expenditure as a proportion of total household spending in a country. In a country with a high Engel coefficient, people have to work in order to live from hand to mouth, being left with limited means for leisure and entertainment. The Engel coefficient for China was 63.9%[1] in 1978. 40 years later, it dropped had

---

[1] http://www.chinadaily.com.cn/business/chinaecoachievement40years/index.html

© Springer Nature Switzerland AG 2020
J. Y. Yang, *The Pricing Puzzle*, https://doi.org/10.1007/978-3-030-50777-0_22

to 28.4%,[2] in 2018. I was fortunate to live through this remarkable period of transition, never really having to worry about my way of living. Although Chinese people are no longer as dependent on food prices as they used to be, conversations about the prices of what comes to the dining table continued as always. Just as the Chinese have liked to talk about food throughout their entire known history, the controversial price hikes of garlic, onions and pork, etc. in recent years also present themselves as delightful conversation starters.

Notwithstanding the occasional price irregularities, one cannot overlook a steady price increase trend in China; just as in many other fast growing countries, most evidently this is the case for fast-moving consumer goods. Take milk as an example. As I commuted between Germany and China on a regular basis in the last decade, I witnessed the diverging development of price of in these two countries. The contrast is nothing short of spectacular. In the last decade, the price of a one liter pack of fresh milk rose from €1 to more than €4 in China, as average Chinese consumers grew more and more acquainted with dairy products and became ready to pay for premium products. Manufacturers responded with more diversified products and specialty products, which further fueled the premiumization of the diary product industry. In the same time period in Germany, dairy product prices stayed stable, fluctuating around €1 with a relatively small margin. As milk is a must-have product, most revenues are realized at the *market price*, by which I mean that there is little price differentiation across different brands at major grocery stores. Any abrupt price changes guaranteed a news mention on the cover page of a German mainstream newspaper. Conformity prevails in the diary product market in Germany. Consequently, the brand and product variety is almost identical as 10 years ago. Similarities are found in many other product categories such as that of coffee or that of utensils, and also nutrition products, and so on, where prices have barely changed over years. Expat friends of mine, who have been living in Shanghai for a long time, told me in amazement how drastically the things could change in such a short period of time: "we used to pack our bags full when visiting home while in Europe and then return with an empty bag. Today, the opposite has becomes true. Living expenses for expats have gotten so high that we have started to take things from Europe to Shanghai."

How come the price trend is so markedly different in these two countries? How do those poor Chinese people cope with the ever-increasing prices? Is this disparity in the price trend going to continue?

---

[2] http://en.people.cn/n3/2019/0221/c90000-9548329.html

There are no simple answers to the questions above. Nevertheless, one obvious explanation lies in the different stages of economic growth of Germany vs. China. Intuitively, in a developed economy like that of Germany, moderate growth is the norm, while big fluctuation in demand and supply is rather rare. On the other hand, China has been charged with growth, looking for every possible opportunity to accelerate growth. A good year is a year with a two-digit rate growth, although this has become increasingly impossible after decades of fast growth. What does this have to do with price increases?

To begin with, economic expansion usually goes hand in hand with an increase in prices. Recall that price is ultimately determined by the relation between supply and demand. A surplus on the supply side relative to demand puts downward pressure on price, while a surplus in demand relative to supply lifts the price. There are only five possible scenarios of Gross Domestic Product growth, a conventional indicator for economic expansion.[3] These scenarios are as follows:

The economy has …

- … produced more at *higher prices*
- … produced the same amount at *higher prices*
- … produced less at *much higher prices*
- … produced more at the *same prices*
- … produced much more at *lower prices*

… in this year compared to the previous year.
Let's take a closer look at the scenarios.

Scenario 1 witnesses a strong growth of the economy, as demand outstrips supply. Businesses must hire more employees, which leads to an increase in wages, further fueling the process. While supply is catching up, strong demand will force prices to go up.

Scenario 2 is often attributed to cost shock. Suppliers increase prices to pass on the cost increase of key commodities to their customers. Demand is more or less stable in this scenario.

Scenario 3 is known as stagflation, a situation that everyone wants to avoid. The economy is expanding below the desired level, while sustained price increases, also known as inflation, prevail. Unemployment remains high due to a low production level.

---

[3] https://www.investopedia.com/ask/answers/112814/why-does-inflation-increase-gdp-growth.asp

Scenario 4 implies that production is being increased to meet increased demand. Higher production leads to a lower unemployment rate, further fueling demand. Increased wages lead to higher demand as consumers spend more freely. GDP rises, while price may also increase eventually.

Scenario 5 is a scenario that has not been seen in recent times, as no producer is willing to increase production in the face of deflation for an extended period of time.

It should have become clear from this brief overview that a price increase is almost inevitable in an expanding economy which is accompanied by a rise in both demand and supply. As demand expands, we shall expect to see a moderate amount of inflation. As prices rise, we will be able to buy less goods with the money in our pocket. In other words, we will be suffering from a loss of purchasing power. Apparently, average consumers of sound mind will not like price increases for all necessities in their lives. Too abrupt or too fast a price increase will be unsettling for the society. That is the reason why most governments and central banks all over the world keep a close eye on checking and controlling the price increases of consumer goods.

Interestingly enough, governmental bodies may sometimes unwillingly trigger price increases in the market. The Chinese welfare authorities, for example, routinely announce annual salary increase plans for civil servants and retirees several months in advance of their taking effect. Usually, already on the second day, the farmers and merchants on the markets will then increase the prices of vegetables and meat, putting up the argument that the consumers will soon be having more money to spend so that a moderate price increase is totally reasonable and fair. The truth is, however, the *moderate* price increase often turned out to be a double-digit increase in the last years. But the sellers always got away with doing this, for as long as I can recall, judging from my table conversations! Indeed, both consumers and merchants on the market have been conditioned to react to the salary increase plans with increasing prices by accepting these. It is a neat real-life example showcasing how price, the invisible hand of the market, responds to the new arrival of information that may tip the balance of demand and supply in a self-automated process.

Are Chinese consumers too dumb or wealthy enough not to care about price increases anymore? How dare the sellers raise prices before their customers have their salary increases in their pockets? In contrast to this, in Germany, the manufacturers of necessity goods are under close scrutiny by the consumers as well as the media. Even a slight price increase can potentially generate in very unpleasant publicity.

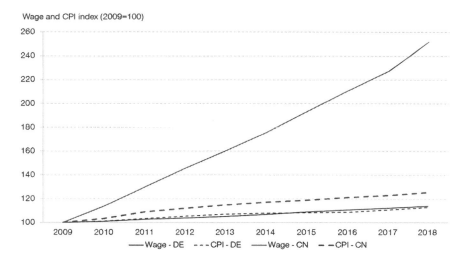

Fig. 1 Wage and CPI index Germany vs. China 2009–2008. (Source: Author's own figure, based on Statista data (https://www.statista.com/statistics/416207/average-annual-wages-germany-y-on-y-in-euros/;   https://www.statista.com/statistics/262859/inflation-rate-in-germany-changes-of-the-cpi-compared-to-the-previous-year/; https://www.statista.com/statistics/743522/china-average-yearly-wages/; https://www.statista.com/statistics/270338/inflation-rate-in-china/); German wage data of 2017 and 2018 were not available and thus estimated based on extrapolation)

Figure 1 should shed some light on the price trends I have seen in Germany and China. I have these from Statista, a German online portal for statistics, data on wages, and the consumer price index, also known as CPI, for both Germany and China, for the ten-year period from 2009 to 2018. For easy comparison and interpretation, I converted both measures into indices, while setting the 2009 numbers to 100 as the baseline.

The eye-catching red solid line depicts the wage trajectory in China, which had an impressive increase of 150% and more. In the meantime, the CPI in China rose *only* by about 25%. Yes, living expenses for average Chinese consumers have been undergoing steady increases. In light of the wage increases, the pains of price increases appear as somehow tolerable growing pains. As one can see from Fig. 1, the wedge shape between wages and the CPI lines has become more pronounced over the years. This means that the net purchasing power of Chinese consumers is on the rise. On a positive note, I would like to think the price increase for foods and everything else is the price that has to be paid for growth, and, more importantly, that it remains a payable one.

Likewise, the two black lines refer to developments in Germany, where wage and CPI have grown almost at the same rate over the last 10 years. In the first half, consumer price inflation even outgrew wage increases. It appears logical that the average German would be more sensitive to price increases than the average Chinese. That which ends up in their pockets makes all the difference here. As long as the economy keeps growing, it is logical to assume that the Chinese consumers would not be bothered much by *moderate* price increases for vegetables and meat.

Quite on the contrary, I have seen cases where people fervently crave price increases. It seems weird at first but entirely human, if you consider the following scenarios: Once we own something, we are inclined to find reasons to justify the ownership, also known as loss aversion in behavioral economics jargon. There is more to it. If the possession is something valuable such as real estate, people actually love to see its price go up year over year, no matter how fiercely they complained about the price at the time of purchase. Humans are known to be inflicted with such dilemmas. And in this one, we may hesitate to make the purchase decision for fear of overpaying. Once we own something, price increases suddenly become okay, as they then prove that we have made the right decision in making the purchase in the first place.

There are certain things in life that we do not like but need in order to keep our lives going. Price increases, or more precisely expressed, reasonable price increases are actually good for all in the long run, despite possible downsides in the short run.

Remember This!

- A moderate price increase/inflation indicates that the economy is doing well.
- Consumers are more likely to accept a price increase, when their income increase outgrows price increase, which can be seen as the price for growth.
- We should be happy that price increases moderately over time.

The Moral of Pricing

What You Will Discover?

As one can imagine, it is a difficult topic for a pricing consultant. Generally, we would encourage clients to defend or increase prices, as price decreases usually do not pay off financially. But there are also difficult times like the COVID-19 pandemic, in which we are reluctant about making any recommendation to increase prices, as many businesses are on the brink of bankruptcy. Maintaining price integrity is critical to any business. The flip side is that customers will have to pay more. Where are the boundaries of pricing ethics?

When I started my career at Simon-Kucher & Partners, the pricing consultancy, a dozen years ago, it was also kind of new to me that price could be actively managed. And I have to confess that in the early years of my price consulting career, I was often plagued by the following questions:

* *Is what I am doing moral?*
* *Am I helping manufacturers in ripping off poor consumers?*
* *Is it fair to charge higher prices?*

Once I got pissed off, when I learned that some of my colleagues were starting a pricing project for a local supermarket chain where I usually do my grocery shopping. As long as I can recall, our pricing projects usually led to price increases. I was afraid that my grocery bills would increase in the foreseeable future.

For years I found it difficult to come to peaceful terms with the different roles that I play, that of being a pricing consultant on the one hand and that of being a consumer on the other. I even thought of writing about pricing

© Springer Nature Switzerland AG 2020
J. Y. Yang, *The Pricing Puzzle*, https://doi.org/10.1007/978-3-030-50777-0_23

ethics in my doctoral dissertation but did not follow through with that idea in the end. Along the way, I also came to understand that finding the right price is of vital importance for any going concern. Price underpins a firm's strategy as to what customer segments the firm is addressing. Ultimately, the price, not the cost, determines the prospects of a firm. From a consumer point of view, price optimization by the supplier is not necessarily bad news either. After the pricing project for the supermarket chain just mentioned, several products that I frequently bought there to my relief became even cheaper. Good pricing practice is always a delicate balance between value provision (the product or service) and value extraction (the price). It is, after all, not evil to demand an appropriate price.

That being said, it remains a tricky and sensitive task to define the moral limits of price. Remember the incident in London in 2017 when people got furious to find out that Uber increased car sharing fares during a terror attack? No matter whether we like it or not, there will be uncomfortable pricing moments in our personal lives.

Consider another example: Smoking is banned in hotel rooms in many places nowadays. Violation of the rule will lead to a hefty fine—it would cost the smoker ¥500 in Beijing, up to HK$5000 in Hong Kong, €250 in Frankfurt, and $200 in New York. Occasionally, I was able to smell traces of smoke in a non-smoking hotel room. How could that be? Why would people do it despite there being clearly visible no smoking signs in the room? I guessed it was because of the fine, which is a price in disguise, to have been an invitation to the smoker. The very existence of a price tag suggests that it is something that can actually be bought. It is ironic. The fine is supposed to prevent someone from smoking. In reality, it may actually encourage smoking, if someone attaches greater value to smoking than to paying the fine.

In his book *What Money Can't Buy*, Harvard Professor Michael J. Sandel points out that "…When we decide that certain goods may be bought and sold, then we decide—at least implicitly—that it is appropriate to treat them as commodities, as instruments of profit and use. But not all goods are properly valued in this way. The most obvious example is human beings" (Sandel Michael 2012).

Many years ago, Mr. X, a member of the senior management at my former employer, was giving an improvised speech at an informal company meeting. As it happened, he brought his newly married young wife to the event. Some female co-workers eyed her bling-bling engagement ring and wowed with great excitement. Mr. X calmed down the audience and gave a piece of advice to the young male colleagues, which I still vividly remember to date: "Do you know how much money you should spend on the engagement ring? Simple. As a rule of thumb, the price of the engagement ring should be the equivalent of three months' salaries." I am pretty sure that he meant well, but is it right to attach a price tag to our affection? It is a terrifying thought. If you do not follow the rule, you may end up risking losing the love of your life. Love is at stake (although you should also know that it is not true love if you lose some-one over a diamond).

In more precarious cases such as life-saving drugs, if one cannot afford the price, lives are at stake. International pharmaceutical companies are often accused of charging too high prices so that patients in need cannot afford the medication, while they defend themselves by saying that the high prices are a sine qua non in order to fund costly and lengthy research and development. In the meantime, medical drugs belong to the product categories for which we see the widest variation on a global scale. Americans often pay at least twice of what patients in other developed countries pay for the exact same drug,[1] so that the lowering of drug prices is among the US President Trump's recurring Twitter topics. In another part of the world, India is known to be a master at finding the right balance between protecting intellectual property rights and satisfying its people's healthcare needs. Prior to 2005, no patent was granted on medicines in India.[2] Do some people deserve better medical treatment than the others, treatment which could mean either life or death? We would instantly say no. It goes without saying that the reality behind this sees this differently.

Dr. Jörg Reinhardt, Chairman of the Board of Directors at Novartis offered his vision of a solution:

> We firmly believe that therapies should be paid on the basis of their value. We are determined to set our prices according to this principle. In the future, costs for a genetic therapy will be justified by their value for the individual patient.

As a matter of fact, such principles have made inroads into our life. In Cologne, for example, the fees for day care in a municipally funded kinder-garten are linked to the income level of the parents. The higher the total income of the household is, the higher the fees will it be. I don't know whether this is fair at all, though it is accepted. In a similar vein, tax authorities in many countries adhere to a progressive tax scheme linked to income level. It is not unusual for super rich people to give up their citizenship and flee to tax havens. If the abovementioned practices are acceptable, the idea of linking drug price to individual wealth seems worth entertaining.

Partly under pressure from governmental authorities, pharmaceutical com-panies are increasingly exploring alternative pricing models in addition to

---

[1] https://eu.usatoday.com/story/news/health/2020/02/06/trump-and-drug-prices-state-of-the-union-prescription-reform-pass/4470776002/.

[2] https://www.iiprd.com/pharmaceutical-patents-a-threat-to-indias-drug-industry/.

outright payments. For example, under the umbrella of so-called Patient Assistance Programs (PAPs), pharmaceutical companies fund charitable organizations and work with hospitals and distributors to provide free or discounted drugs to patients having successfully applied for the program.

At the turn of year 2019/2020, a new coronavirus disease, officially dubbed COVID-19, first erupted in Wuhan, a Chinese metropolis with a population of more than 11 million inhabitants. Soon it quickly spread across mainland China and then spread to overseas, also as the outbreak coincided with the massive human traffic over the Chinese New Year holiday. To contain the escalating risk of infection, governmental authorities by mandate instructed the people to wear surgical masks in public. Failure to do became punishable. Masks were in severe shortage. Amid the fear of catching COVID-19, people went crazy about getting masks from every possible channel. The most wanted Chinese New Year gifts in 2020 were surgical masks. Some pharmacies made money from the opportunity by charging ten times the regular price. Mask prices were a hot topic in vox populi. While we condemn the pricing policies of unscrupulous merchants, should not we also consider that costs were also significantly increasing due to the forced shutdown of production sites? A reasonable price increase may well be necessary to enable a sufficient supply of masks being available in time. In time of emergency, is letting the invisible hand regulating prices still superior to rigid governmental intervention? These are just some of the hard questions we seek answers to. I believe the debate on the moral of pricing will persist. It comes down to the perception of fairness. Especially in extreme situations which we cannot foresee, we just have no clue at all about what is fair. Even if we do, our opinions will likely remain divided.

Remember This!

- It is not evil to demand an appropriate price, which is a quality stamp for value provided.
- Good pricing practice can be a win-win situation, where the seller can discern customer groups with different needs and correspondingly a different level in willingness to pay.
- In the end, the moral of pricing concerns the perception of fairness, which is subjective and can be controversial at times.

Reference

Sandel Michael J (2012) What money can't buy: the moral limits of markets. Farrar, Straus and Giroux, New York

Price in Pieces

Originally I wanted to use the title *Price in pieces* for this book. I got the inspiration from an American comedy show *Life in Pieces* that I watched years ago. My editor talked me out of it in the end. But I really like the sound of the title I had first wanted to use. Therefore, I allowed myself to use it as the title for this chapter to review some of the fun/uncanny moments that I had when conversing with clients, colleagues and friends. What I am trying to say is that we encounter pricing all the time, even if we do not immediately recognize these moments as pricing moments. These encounters are scattered, unstructured, in pieces. In what follows, you will find below a selection of my personal repertoire of pricing dialogues.

I separate the dialogues into two categories, respectively *at work* and *off work*, and try to put them in a logical sequence. Spoiler alert: there is not always science behind each dialogue. Whether pricing is science or art is still debatable. Therefore I highlighted the keywords as reading aids at the end of each dialogue to highlight what the key messages are.

At Work: The Pricing Consultant Side of Me

Question #1 Why shall we conduct market research? Steve Jobs never did any market research. Yet he created the iPhone, which is such a great product.

The short answer: First, we do not know 100% whether it is true. Second, how dare you say you are as good as Steve Jobs?

© Springer Nature Switzerland AG 2020
J. Y. Yang, *The Pricing Puzzle*, https://doi.org/10.1007/978-3-030-50777-0_24

The unsaid: What we know for sure is that Steve Jobs was an exceptional genius. The 1% geniuses are always entitled to privileges—they do whatever they want, and whatever they do turns out to be alright, most of the time. The remaining 99% of people are be better off following the best practices. Doing market research is like a no-brainer. Should you conduct some sort of market research before launching a project? Definitely! It gives you the assurance that you are doing the right thing. It gives you a second chance to correct any mistakes, before you go all in and fail. Market research is a cost-effective way to glean customer insights and is thus strongly recommended.

It goes without saying that market research does not get you to come up with a 100% perfect product. But it will help you to score say 80%, if you do it correctly. The remaining 20% requires luck and ingenuity. The great late Jobs was an exception. Exceptions prove the rules.

The owner of a design bag startup once shared with me a real story of his. Every time his company is about to launch a new product, the product and marketing teams will gather together to assess the prospects of the product in question. A while ago, there was this "ugly" bag on the table for joint evaluation. Almost everyone dismissed the bag. But it got approved due to the persistence of the designer. Guess what? It turned to be one of the best sellers of the year for the company.

It was a revealing shock to the entire team but it also taught them a valuable lesson. We are all biased, believe it or not. When it comes to new product development, it is imperative to get out of one's own shoes and try to see the product through the eyes of the customers. To that end, market research is a useful tool.

Keywords: Market research; New product pricing

Question #2 Can you make an educated guess about the pricing maturity of a company after just a glimpse?

The short answer: I would make that decision based on whether the company has a dedicated pricing function and how high up that function is situated in the organizational hierarchy.

The unsaid: We pricing consultants often suggest that pricing belongs to the boardroom. There is evidence from Simon-Kucher's global pricing survey that firms achieve better profit margins if the senior management is involved in pricing. Unfortunately, in reality this is more often than not not the case. According to a desk research conducted in 2019, there are more than 70,000 pricing job listings in the United States, about 700 of these in Germany and, strikingly, less than 70 in China. It seems that the more mature an economy is, the greater emphasis the companies will put on pricing. Many organizations do not even have a dedicated pricing function, leaving it to the invisible hand of the market, or they follow their competitors' pricing. It is no different to letting your competitors manage your business. Despite how crazy it may sound, many companies are actually doing that, burying their heads in sand.

Keywords: *Pricing maturity; Pricing manager*

Question #3 The concept of value pricing resonates with me very much. But the market situation opposes it. All my competitors are so irrational and set their focus on protecting market shares. Does value pricing also work in a highly competitive environment like mine?

The short answer: Yes. You should definitely watch out for competitors' moves. But it is the wrong place to start if you start with your pricing. To capture full price potential, you need to think first what value you bring to your customers.

The unsaid: There is a recurring question in Simon-Kucher's annual global pricing survey, which asks about who it is that starts the price war in the industry that is being participated in. The quota has been consistently over 60%, which means the majority believes it is the others' fault. Price war is like a downward spiral. Once it gets started, everyone is hurt by it. There is usually no winner at the end of a price war.

Frankly speaking, a competitive market situation does make the practice of value pricing more difficult, as aggressive price actions will take a heavy toll on the customers' willingness to pay. A company that nurtures a value-first mentality will gain a competitive edge over the rest. For one thing, not all customers are equally price-sensitive, even in a harsh environment. It is not necessary to offer low prices simply everywhere; another aspect is that value pricing helps the companies discover unmet customer needs which opens doors to new opportunities.

A photo studio specialized in kids photo shooting had been struggling in acquiring new customers ever since it started. To be on the "safe" side, management set the prices at a similar level as those of its competitors and ran promotions on a regular basis. But the demand was lukewarm, and the studio could barely make ends meet. Partly out of desperation, the CEO took the decision to step up the offering and charge a significant premium to set it apart from the me-too competition. It worked! The studio is making remarkable progress in both revenue and profit.

Last but not least, if your company is a market leader, you should be (held) responsible for maintaining the price level in the market. The reason is straightforward. All others are looking up to you. If you cut prices, the others will probably follow suit.

Keywords: *Commodity trap; Leadership*

Question #4 What is your take on the pursuit of price value relationship?

The short answer: I think it is a false proposition.

The unsaid: Pursuit of a superior price value relationship is the mantra in many companies, especially for newcomers. There are two levers that can be used in order to improve the price value relationship. One can either decrease the cost to achieve a better price or invest to improve customer value. Obviously, the two levers are in conflict. It would be too naive to believe that you can have them both in the long run. Some companies which root for price value relationship claim to provide the best value for the price they charge. The statement sounds fair but is a compromise in disguise. The conflict between "lower cost/better price" and "improved customer value" persists. When the conflict manifests itself and is becoming difficult to be reconciled, guess which lever gets the upper hand? According to my experience, it is always lower cost/better price. Why? Because it is easier to implement.

Consequently, I have come to automatically react with aversion when someone extols the magic expression of price value relationship. I tend to interpret it as a sign of lacking strategic direction.

Chinese tech unicorn Xiaomi is well-known as an advocate of the price value relationship. Mr. Lei, the CEO, even made public its 5% profit margin policy on hardware to prove that. However, the company has always been struggling with the speed to market. The latest flagship, Mi phones, as well as popular accessories is always difficult to get after the release. Waiting times may span months, which is not something eager Chinese consumers will tolerate. There was suspicion that Xiaomi was doing this on purpose to create a sense of scarcity, of sought-after products in order to stimulate consumer's appetite. However, Mr. Lei never admitted to this accusation as being correct.

I pre-ordered a higher-range model of the Mi Smart Watch in December 2019, and it was still out of stock at the beginning of March 2020. That is inacceptable. I started to believe what looks like marketing hunger was actually not happening on purpose. It seems that Xiaomi has difficulty in getting its supply chain in line with demand. Owing to its sustained low price strategy (high value-price ratio strategy in official terms), Xiaomi must have been giving the upstream suppliers a hard time. Guess which client the suppliers will favor in case there are production constraints? The stingy Xiaomi or generous Apple?

PS After waiting for three hopeless months, I removed the smartwatch from my shopping basket. It is not as if I do not any have other choices.

Keywords: Price; Value; Compromise

Question #5 Did you ever fail in your pricing projects?

The short answer: No, I did not fail.

The unsaid: I don't know why I get this kind of question all the time. I am not sure whether the client is looking for assurance for or a reason to turn down my proposal.

But have I really never failed? Well, it depends on the definition of failure. Pricing projects do not yield a 50% profit increase every single time they happen. However, the downside is also limited. In the worst case, the client learns how to manage pricing in a more structured way. The payoff will be long-lasting, even if it cannot be realized immediately due to market conditions or internal constraints. Thereby, it is just a matter of the magnitude of the impact. I like to quote one of my favorite clients who responded to my invitation to a meeting for discussing follow-up initiatives:

"The project that your team delivered was fantastic. You created real value for us. But we do not intend to work with you in the foreseeable future. Good consultants are like poison. I do not want my people to become addicted and to stop thinking for themselves."

Bad for him, bad for us. Building pricing competence is like building muscles. Having a good coach alongside is invaluable.

Keywords: Failure; Pricing muscles

Question #6 We would love to work with you on this project. But what you ask is way beyond our expectation. Could you give us more discounts?

The short answer: Sorry, I cannot. I will be discounting my credibility if I give you more discounts. How can I help you with your pricing when I cannot do my own right?

The unsaid: My viewpoint is that if the client truly believes in the value of our work, she or he is willing to pay for it. Mutual trust is the foundation for successful cooperation. I hate preaching wine while drinking water. I like and need to walk the talk. Pricing integrity matters. This kind of question usually signals that I am talking to the wrong customer.

Keywords: Pricing integrity

Question #7 (During a client acquisition meeting someone whose identity was unknown at that time was asking:) What constitutes great pricing? The overall suitability or minimizing errors between forecast and actuals for individual customers?

The short answer: Pricing needs to be fair and easy to communicate. By the way, are you a data scientist?

The unsaid: While I was listening to myself responding to his question, it became clear to me what he was actually driving at. He was concerned with the output for individual outliers in a dynamic pricing model driven by machine learning. A statistically sound model might perform very well on aggregate level, but it cannot rule out unfortunate cases in which some individuals stand to be severely disadvantaged. Setting restriction rules would not be always practical, as too many exceptions break integrity of the algorithm. That is where probably the limits of technology still lie.

The moment he raised the question, I had strong instinct that this guy must be a data scientist (or a nerd). He turned out to be a new hire on the data science team and was charged with the task of upgrading the pricing algorithm to set initial property prices.

Keywords: Pricing fairness; Machine learning

Question #8 What? You are a pricing consultant? Isn't price determined by the market?

The short answer: You don't want to entrust your fate to the invisible hand.

The unsaid: Usually my older Chinese friends would ask me this question. Only in hindsight did I realize the irony. Given their communist background, shouldn't they ask "Isn't price determined by labor cost?" At least Karl Marx was of the opinion.

Now, joke aside. According to Adam Smith, the invisible hand finds an equilibrium between supply and demand and in turn determines the price. However, price search takes time. The first mover has the advantage of setting the price anchor in the market, which has substantial influence on the lifetime value of the product in question. Pricing consultants**Error! Bookmark not defined.** add value by helping companies get the pricing starting line right.

For the price optimization of existing products, you would also use pricing consultants. The equilibrium price abovementioned is an averaged value, which means that there are deviations. Pricing consultants supported the price adjustment, maximizing value along a product's cycle.

Keywords: Pricing profession

Question #9 What traits are you looking for when hiring a new pricing consultant? Any preferences for educational background or work experience?

The short answer: Actually, very simple. You need to look smart...and be smart.

The unsaid: Honestly speaking, pricing is not rocket science. But it has many facets, inextricably connected internally with cross-functional teams and requiring a sharp sense of insight into the customer. It is a complex task, bridging the inside (the organization) and the outside (the market), and one that ultimately determines how profitable the firm will be. It really does not matter what educational background or what work experience you have; what matters is that you are levelheaded about what is going on and able to bridge the gap between value (what is offered to the customers) and price (what is demanded by customers in exchange).

Keywords: *Look smart; Be smart*

Question #10 What is your pricing advice for companies in a sentence?

The answer: Price should equate value. Do not shy away from claiming your deserved price. I constantly get the feeling that the customers are actually expecting their suppliers to ask for a higher price if they are satisfied with the product or service.

Keywords: *Do not shy away*

Off Work: The Consumer Side of Me

Question #11 Is pricing art or science?

The short answer: It is both.

The unsaid: This is one of the rare moments in which I can give a clear answer without dodging it in a consultant-typical way by saying "It depends." Pricing comes down to numbers. There cannot be good pricing decisions without some number crunching, as is typical of any science known to man. However, as so often, humans make decisions last. We can factor in the X factor of human behavior to a certain extent. Nevertheless, I am convinced that no model can capture all factors that influence pricing in the real world. Although there are simulation models that can precisely tell you the odds of pricing outcomes, we all sometimes just believe that we can do better than machines. How and when do we deviate from machine-generated suggestions? Answering that question is definitely art.

My word of advice: side with the science if you need to pick one. To err is human.

Keywords: *Pricing art; Pricing science*

Question #12 Have you ever fallen into a price trap?

The short answer: Hm, a couple of times I guess.

The unsaid: Behind the modesty there is something that I am not particularly proud of. My professional training makes me more sensible to the pricing happening all around me, but it does not make me immune to pricing traps, even though I should know better. I am, for instance, as I see it, a lousy consumer.

On a sunny weekend afternoon, Doreen and I took the kids to the park. We were playing football on the central lawn, and then the kids spotted some other kids were playing bubble guns so that they also wanted them. I went to the kiosk next to the lawn to buy the bubble guns. I paid 20 RMB for a plastic bubble gun without even trying to haggle over the price. The bubble guns were fun; it took 10 min at the most until the soap had been used up. Doreen did not stop me but instead laughed about me for paying the exorbitant prices on the way back home. To prove that I was an idiot, she searched for bubble guns on Taobao.com, a B2C/C2C marketplace owned by Alibaba.com. It turned out that you could get a dozen of those plastic toys for 60 RMB. I had paid four times the regular price. Did I regret it? Yes, maybe for a second. But the smiles on the kids' faces were priceless for me.

Once I had to travel to a client by train who was in a remote location. Upon arrival at the departing railway station, I found that I still had some time for a quick bite. All the popular restaurants were busy, with long queues of those waiting at the counter to place orders. I am really not a fan of queuing, especially as I have this uncanny capability of picking the queue with the longest waiting time. So I settled for a less popular fast-food chain restaurant. I wanted a burger and a drink but ended up leaving the counter with a prepaid loyalty card featuring freebies and discount coupons. I should have known better that I would overestimate my need for consumption and that the purchase did not make sense. But I was not that rational and bought it anyway. Who does not like a bargain? Colleagues laughed at me when they found out what I had done. And they were right. There were so many constraints attached that I would be able to use only less than half of the coupons before the expiration date of the loyalty card. In retrospect, the cashier was really convincing. My takeaway: good pricing does not sell itself. Good sales does.

Keywords: *Price traps; Good sales*

Question #13 (My wife Doreen says) We are moving soon. Let's put the old sideboard on eBay Kleinanzeigen (a C2C classified ad service provided by eBay in Germany). As it is just an IKEA product, shall we just set the price to zero to get rid of it as soon as possible?

The short answer: We won't become rich by selling a sideboard. But let's still ask for something like 5 Euro to avoid weirdos.

The unsaid: Zero price is equal to zero value. Buyers will not take you seriously because they have nothing to lose. Another side effect of offering something for free is indeed that you may run into some strange people.

A few days after my conversation with Doreen, a friend of ours told us a story. She had a bookshelf to spare and put it on eBay Kleinanzeigen for free. The buyer, or, more precisely, the taker, soon came by, showing up punctually to pick up the bookshelf. Before he left, he asked whether she could give him 10 Euro to fill his fuel tank. What a scam!

The same friend was giving away a TV set for free the other time. During the inquiry about the specifications, the potential buyer accused her of not being polite and dropped the deal. These bizarre encounters really drove her nuts. I hope that she has learned a lesson at least. As far as we are concerned, I am glad that we did not give away our sideboard for free. Bad pricing invites bad luck.

Keywords: *Zero price; Zero value; Bad luck*

Question #14 What do you think of small prints, also known as hidden terms and conditions?

The short answer: I absolutely hate them as a consumer, while I have to admit that from a business perspective, they do make sense.

The unsaid: Small prints are hideous and conceal terms and conditions that are detrimental to customers, a practice commonly used by utilities and telecom companies among others. The classic tricks include a default price increase after a certain time period, an extremely long notice period for contract termination, and automatic contract renewal, just to name a few. Customers tend to fall into the trap as they rush to fill out and sign an order, or they simply ignore the small print; customers hate it when they find out that they have been tricked. But when all suppliers have the same small print policy, customers have only themselves to blame for having not been more attentive.

By the way, small print seems to be more widespread and accepted in Germany than anywhere else for reasons that I do not know. Is Germany really a service desert?

#SmallPrints #MadeInGermany #ServiceDesert

Question #16 What is your favorite worst-of-pricing example?

The short answer: You mean what pricing examples I hate? This one is easy. It is the smartwatch maker W (I had better not disclose the name).

The unsaid: Being a big fan of Bauhaus, I love the W concept and its sleek design language. The smart part of the watch is also user-friendly—for starters, you do not have to press any button to tell the watch what activities you are about to engage in. The sensor will guess what is happening and record your performance automatically. So, quite cool stuff.

As an absolutely early adopter, I have owned at least five timepieces from this tech startup since its inception. Despite there having been promotions frequently, I have miraculously managed to buy all of mine at full price. Nevertheless, there are annoying moments when the devices fail to do what they are supposed to do or the connection between the watch and the smartphone breaks down. To my relief, their customer service staff is both accommodating and competent. I do appreciate that.

But W sucks at marketing and pricing. The worst of all is its mailing campaign. I proactively check in on the website to see what is new from time to time. As a subscriber to W's newsletter, I also receive promotional emails on a regular basis. Some of the emails are literally unnerving. After I had purchased and then had a new model for no more than 2 months, I received an email from W informing me of the great news that my recently purchased timepiece was on promotion right now! This has happened a couple of times already. Does W do this on purpose to alienate loyal customers like me? Sadly, I continue to buy new watches from W.

Keywords: Worst of pricing

Question #15 What is your favorite best-of-pricing example?

The short answer: I do not have one yet.

The unsaid: Honestly, I believe we can always do better. The next will be better. But I do have a few candidates for the best pricing award (in alphabetic order):

1. iPhone by Apple—Apple remains triumphant in the modern smartphone era though applying a skimming pricing strategy. Moving further into the life cycle, it defends its market/premium price position with expensive flagship models and supplies the lower end of the market with obsolescent models priced at significantly lower price levels. It does a very good job at price fencing. In addition, it also does an excellent job at designing the product portfolio, fostering user habits to its benefit while extracting willingness to pay along the way. Just take lightning as an example. Apple reduced the ports to one universal port years ago, which serves both as a charging port and a headphone jack. As a result, more and more iPhone users buy AirPods, and various adapters, if they wish to continue to use the old accessories. And yes, I remember I discussed earlier how flawed iPhone pricing is.

2. Nespresso by Nestlé—Nespresso epitomizes a continuous ecosystem type of innovation both in technology and for its price model. Nespresso fundamentally changed the way coffee was made and consumed at home, at work, and on the road. The capsuled coffee thrived as a new product category and convinced consumers around the world of its supreme quality, which helped the significant price premium. The division between professional and private use by means of a differentiated product design and price model is textbook-like price fencing.

3. Netflix by Netflix—Netflix was already a classic case study when I attended my MBA program back in 2007. The case study was about how Netflix revolutionized the American DVD rental market. Among others, the subscription model was a key differentiator and growth driver. Netflix reinvented itself in 2010, transforming itself into becoming an online streaming service provider. Netflix revamped its business model. But the subscription model has survived and has been being optimized since then. I am amazed how agilely Netflix tests and rolls out new price schemes in different regions of the world. Chapeau!

4. Hand sanitizer by Rotunden—Rotunden is a Danish grocery market chain. Amid the COVID-19 pandemic in early 2020, disinfectants, toilet paper, and flour among others were constantly in shortage. It was getting close to impossible to buy them at drugstores or supermarkets. The constantly empty shelves reinforced the sense of scarcity and triggered further hoarding. Whoever moved faster got the supplies, leaving other people in need high and dry. Many German supermarkets did what they were used to, i.e., putting up signs which said three units per head per purchase. Did it work? No, as we already knew from the milk formula story. Rotunden did something different and ingenious. It also put up a sign on the shelf of

hand sanitizers. Instead of imposing purchase volume restrictions, it said the following: "40 kr for the first bottle and 1000 kr for every bottle that follows."[1] Since then, things have returned to normal.

Keywords: *Best of pricing*

Question #17 What is your pricing advice for consumers?

The answer: Buy it. Life is short. Do not let the price get in your way. You have many more important things to regret than having paid too high a price.

Keywords: *Buy it; Life is short*

---

[1] 1 DKK = 0.13 EUR, exchange rate per 21st March, 2020

The Pricing Stories Continue

This piece contains the quintessential messages that I would like to bring across to the readers of this book. I have been telling bits of the pricing stories I lived through or observed over the years. It is a learning process for me too to reflect in retrospect on my belief in regard to what price is really about. Why bother caring about pricing, if we know that in most cases the market is going to find the right one anyway? Price management is not confined to just pricing as such. Instead, price management should be seen as active value management. At the end of the day, customers only make the purchase when the perceived value of the goods in questions is equal to or greater than the sacrifice, which is the price they have to pay. It is a kind of equivalence that you find out about through repeated trial and error, or by means of a more structured price finding method. The value added by pricing consultants lies in helping one to find the sweet spot of the price-value equilibrium more quickly.

The idea to orient toward the market price is appealing. Resembling a black box in various aspects, the market is a complex mechanism known to have many unknowns. Isn't it a nice thing to be able to take one big unknown out of the equation and to then just follow the market's wisdom and stay focused on other important tasks needed for keeping a business up and running? Unfortunately, this is no more than wishful thinking. For starters, it is debatable whether such a thing as *the* market price exists.

The market price we learn about during the economics course at college on demand and supply can be elusive as well as illusionary. While the market equilibrium does exist, it masks the fact that every transaction is in somewhat different, involving different customers in different situations. Every buyer

© Springer Nature Switzerland AG 2020
J. Y. Yang, *The Pricing Puzzle*, https://doi.org/10.1007/978-3-030-50777-0_25

has a different value perception, just as every seller. We learn that the crossing point of the demand and supply curve tells us the market price, to be precise, the average market price, which comes out as the average price of thousands or millions of individual transactions. In other words, every participant can influence the market price in a way. In adhering to the market price, or more precisely the prices of competitors, you effectively no longer take part in the quest for excellence. Failure to act on the uniqueness of your customers leads to mediocrity, the fate of a price taker.

Even more importantly, business owners should take pricing seriously because of the net present value (NPV) of pricing. The fact is that no matter how great a product is, it has a finite shelf life. During this limited lifetime period, the prime years will contribute the lion's share to the revenue and profits, while residual value toward the end of this time period threatens to fall swiftly. Therefore, it is imperative to get pricing right early on.

The law of natural selection dictates that everything in this world will be superseded with something greater one day in the future. When Benz and Daimler respectively invented the world's first automobile a hundred years ago, few people thought they would need it. After all, what could beat a fast horse? History repeats itself all the time. Traditional car makers had not taken Tesla and electrical mobility seriously enough. Tesla is now the most valuable US car maker of all time with a market capitalization of $81.4 billion, surpassing Ford Motor's 1999 record of $80.8 billion.[1]

Steven Sasson, a 24-year-old engineer, invented digital photographing technology in 1975 while working at Eastman Kodak. Kodak's management was too comfortable with the traditional film business and let the invention sit at the back of the oven for decades.[1] When they finally realized that the days of film were numbered, it was too late, and the company ended up in bankruptcy (Ramanujam and Tacke 2016). And then again, who would have foreseen that digital cameras would also be short-lived, as smartphones emerged with ever improving photo shooting capabilities? In 2010, the sale of digital cameras reached its peak, when 121 million devices were shipped annually worldwide. The following years saw a decline in shipments across the world. Till the end of 2018, the annual global shipment plummeted to less than 20 million, i.e., merely one-sixth of the peak volume in 2010. According to estimates made by Canon, the market for digital cameras will shrink further, namely, by a half, in the next 2 years.[2]

---

[1] https://www.wsj.com/articles/tesla-is-now-the-most-valuable-u-s-car-maker-of-all-time-11578427858.
[2] https://www.huxiu.com/article/325552.html.

Sometimes existing products become obsolete not even because of direct competitors. Instant noodles are a case in point. Instant noodles are a very popular meal supplement in China and other countries in Southeastern Asia. The sales had been increasing steadily with a two-digit growth rate for two decades till it leveled out in 2013. In 2016, sales in China dropped to 38.5 billion packs, down 17% from the peak in 2013. All manufacturers of instant noodles had to cope with continuous decline in sales. The struggle of instant noodles manufacturers coincided with the rise of food delivery service providers such as Meituan Dianping and Ele.me in the period of 2013–2016. They have fundamentally changed or facilitated the change of the millennials' lifestyles. As food express delivery provides a much broader choice of culinary options at an affordable price and speed, instant noodles have inevitably been marginalized by this despite various efforts.

There are different philosophies of pricing. In practice, every enterprise pursues a somewhat different pricing strategy on the spectrum from pure cost-plus pricing to value-based pricing. The Hidden Champions are usually on the side of value-based pricing. As Hermann Simon will put it, Hidden Champions are small- to medium-sized companies which are worldwide leaders in their niche markets. They succeed and thrive by being close to their customers, providing them with products and service suited to their needs at the same time, profiting from this. By behaving this way, the Hidden Champions can actually drive market share and profitability simultaneously and, more importantly, in a way that can last for years, decades, and even centuries. This is what I call sustainable pricing or *price to last*.

The attitude of Hidden Champions toward market share and pricing results in good market shares and healthy margins, which are achieved through superior quality, innovation, and service. Hidden Champions succeed not only in getting for themselves the lion's share within their markets but also in securing a price premium that is estimated to surpass that of their peers by 10–15% on average (Simon and Yang 2019). Market shares go down when they are acquired through aggressive pricing or promotions, as a consequence of which, margins are bad or even negative, as we have frequently seen happen in the case of startups in recent years.

There is nothing wrong with temporary aggressive pricing. In the early stage, the most important task of a startup is usually to scale up to a critical mass in a timely fashion. In the meantime, one should be wary of the consequences of aggressive pricing for two reasons. Firstly, you might onboard customers who would not be clients without the low price. Once the price returns to the normal level, they will turn their back on you. Secondly, you cannot prevent others from undercutting you in price. If the market environment goes into a "tit-for-tat" mode, there will be no winner at the end of the day. Market shares acquired by aggressive pricing are vulnerable. Throughout my entire pricing consulting career, there have been only a few instances in which I recommended plain price decreases. I am of the opinion that a problem that can be solved by just lowering price is a small one. Value carries a larger weight than price in the customers' purchase decisions. Empirically, price accounts for only 20–50% in importance, the rest being customer perceived value. This means that the sacrifice in price must be over-proportionally high so as to compensate for the gap in value. It is usually too high a price for any company to afford.

The choice of price is a testimony to potential customers, especially when the quality of the product cannot be judged beforehand. I once came across an entrepreneur, a chemist by training, whose startup was dedicated to developing and marketing herbal cosmetic products. She was very proud and confident about the quality of her products and used these, exclusively, on herself as well. She showed off by asking me to guess how old she was. I had to admit that the anti-aging effect was visible on her face. But then I frowned at her pricing strategy, because there was basically none. What she did was to peg her own pricing in relation to the leading brands in the same product category and then discounting by x percentage, whereas x was based on her gut feeling. As a matter of fact, she was allowing massive discounts for her products of up to about one-third of the prices of the market leaders. Presuming that her products were really as good as she claimed, this was not a smart move. Especially as is the case for high-involvement products such as cosmetics, for choosing which consumers invest considerable amounts of time and effort to figure what product suits them the best, they associate a high price more directly with high quality (examples include the Dyson air dryers and Rimowa travel cases which were mentioned in other parts of this book). It is a game in which the highest pricer (the winner) takes all.

SoftBank's Masayoshi Son, well-known for the stellar returns on his legendary early-stage investment in Jack Ma's fledging Alibaba.com, has reflected on his recent misfortunes with WeWork and Slack and demanded a return to the old-fashioned evaluation method—*the enterprise value should be ultimately determined and measured by the ability of the enterprise concerned to make a profit*.[3] He is not alone in this change of attitude toward looking at the profitability of startups.

---

[3] https://www.aljazeera.com/ajimpact/softbanks-message-entrepreneurs-profits-matter-190927012445097.html.

Entrepreneurs need to think about monetization early on, as early as when they are contemplating the product prototype for the first time. Product managers tend to focus on the product-market fit, i.e., finding the right solution (the product) for the right people (the target segment). How financially successful the venture will be remains unknown. Good product managers take it one step further and ask themselves the following questions:

- Am I serving the right customers?
- How much are they willing to pay for the solution to their problem?
- Is the product being conceived able to fully solve the problem?
- Are there features that should be added or removed to match the potential customers' needs and arguably more importantly their willingness to pay?

Asking the questions above forces the product managers to go beyond product-market fit and strive for product-market-price fit (see Fig. 1). Only the latter can ensure the commercial success of the new product. To provide the best to the customers without knowing how much they are willing to pay for it is divine but not in the best interest of the shareholders or investors. Keeping in frequent contact with potential customers, and testing their willingness to pay at important milestones of product development, is the only way I can think of that can make it right. Remember that the shelf time of any great product is limited. Extensive periods of trial and error may prove to be too costly.

Why would entrepreneurs and business owners still bury their heads in the sand, when they have such a powerful tool as pricing at hand?

John Deighton, Professor Emeritus at Harvard Business School, commented that:

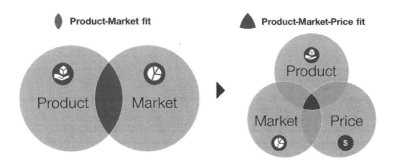

Fig. 1 From product-market fit to product-market-price-fit. (Source: Author's own figure)

When people set a price, they are more sensitive to the downside than they are hungry for the upside. They can think of a thousand ways in which if you price too high, you get into trouble. They don't often enough think of the thousand ways to invest the money they're going to get when they price high. There's a pervasive bias to price below what the market will bear.[4]

I believe that at the end of the day, it is all about choices. We all have choices. Consumers have a choice. Retailers have a choice. Manufacturers have a choice. Price is the yardstick of the choice, the sacrifice. Do not leave it at the mercy of the others.

References

Ramanujam M, Tacke G (2016) Monetizing innovation : how smart companies design the product around the price. Wiley, Hoboken, NJ
Simon H, Yang Y (2019) Hidden Champions, 2nd edn. Industrial Machine Press

---

[4] http://www.msi.org/video/market-making-with-personal-data/.

Index

© Springer Nature Switzerland AG 2020
J. Y. Yang, *The Pricing Puzzle*, https://doi.org/10.1007/978-3-030-50777-0

Druck:
Customized Business Services GmbH
im Auftrag der
KNV Zeitfracht GmbH
Ein Unternehmen der Zeitfracht - Gruppe
Ferdinand-Jühlke-Str. 7
99095 Erfurt